Stories To The Dark

Stories To The Dark

Explorations
in
Religious Imagination

by

William James O'Brien

PAULIST PRESS
New York, N.Y./Ramsey, N.J./Toronto

Cover Design: John Murello
Interior Art: Emil Antonucci

Library of Congress
Catalog Card Number: 77-74577

ISBN: 0-8091-0222-6 (cloth)
ISBN: 0-8091-2032-1 (paper)

Published by Paulist Press
Editorial Office: 1865 Broadway, New York, N.Y. 10023
Business Office: 545 Island Road, Ramsey, N.J. 07446

Printed and bound in the
United States of America

ACKNOWLEDGMENTS

Gratitude is herein expressed to the following publishers for their kind permission to quote from the cited works:

Saint Augustine, CONFESSIONS. Trans. by R. S. Pine-Coffin. Penguin Classics, 1961, pp. 94, 103, 88, 46, 78, 77, 61, 62, 147, 21, 290, 281, 156, 181. Copyright © R. S. Pine-Coffin, 1961. Reprinted by permission of Penguin Books Ltd.

Excerpts from LOST IN THE FUNHOUSE by John Barth. Copyright © 1963, 1966, 1968 by John Barth. Reprinted by permission of Doubleday & Company, Inc., and by the author's agent, Lurton Blassingame.

Bede, A HISTORY OF THE ENGLISH CHURCH AND PEOPLE. Trans. by Leo Sherley-Price. Revised edition, 1968, R. E. Latham, Penguin Classics, 1968. Copyright © Leo Sherley-Price, 1955, 1968. Reprinted by permission of Penguin Books Ltd.

Excerpts from THE DIVINE COMEDY I: HELL by Dante. Trans. by Dorothy L. Sayers. Penguin Classics, 1949. Copyright © the Estate of Dorothy L. Sayers, 1949. Reprinted with permission.

Excerpts from THE DIVINE COMEDY II: PURGATORY by Dante. Trans. by Dorothy L. Sayers. Penguin Classics, 1955. Copyright © the Estate of Dorothy L. Sayers, 1955. Reprinted with permission.

Contents

FOR KAREN

"Your majesty, when we compare the present life of man on earth with that time of which we have no knowledge, it seems to me like the swift flight of a single sparrow through the banqueting-hall where you are sitting at dinner on a winter's day with your thanes and counsellors. In the midst there is a comforting fire to warm the hall; outside, the storms of winter rain or snow are raging. This sparrow flies swiftly in through one door of the hall, and out through another. While he is inside, he is safe from the winter storms; but after a few moments of comfort, he vanishes from sight into the wintry world from which he came. Even so, man appears on earth for a little while; but of what went before this life or of what follows, we know nothing. Therefore, if this new teaching has brought any more certain knowledge, it seems only right that we should follow it."

King's Counsellor to King Edwin, *c.* 625 A.D.
in Bede's *A History of the English Church and People*

Preface

The people who walked in darkness
have seen a great light:
light has dawned upon them,
dwellers in a land as dark as death. (Is. 9:1)

This book, which gestures in the direction of that light, had its beginnings in a course I offered undergraduates at the University of Notre Dame in the spring of 1976. I am, in the first place, indebted to those young men and women for their lively and encouraging response, their wit and their honesty.

I owe a special debt of gratitude to David Burrell, C.S.C., whose initial encouragement persuaded me to compose this manuscript. In the course of writing, I benefited greatly from conversations with Roberta Chesnut and William Storey of the department of theology and Thomas Werge and William Krier of the department of English here at Notre Dame. I also had the great advantage of testing out my rather unusual reading of Dante's *Divine Comedy* in the course of a summer-long discussion with friends from the university, their spouses, and visitors from Emory and Auburn universities. To them I am grateful for bringing to my attention the difficulties besetting the interpretation of Dante

1

I have attempted here. My mistakes are now more fully my own. I might add that the occurrence of discussions like ours is not uncommon in this place. Notre Dame has been for me a singular university, attracting people who create occasions such as these for a devoted and friendly study of great literature. For that I am grateful.

My debt to John S. Dunne, C.S.S., and John Gerber, C.S.C., is more particular, since certain notions I have explored at length in the text I first heard in conversation with them. I think especially of John Dunne's notion of "refusing to fill the void with imagination" and John Gerber's notion of "letting go the images that hold the life" and "accepting in their place images that free the life." Of course I accept full responsibility for the particular ways I have exploited the possibilities resident in these notions.

Finally, I wish to express my thanks to David Burrell, C.S.C., to Stanley Hauerwas, and to my wife Karen, who read the text and offered me valuable criticism. Above all, Karen's judgment of argument and style has benefited these pages. Her encouraging response to the work as it grew meant far more to me because of the frankness and incisiveness of the criticism she offered from the very beginning. Without that special kind of support I doubt I could have brought the work, once begun, to completion.

Christmas, 1976, University of Notre Dame

Introduction

In Rainer Maria Rilke's "A Story Told to the Dark," the narrator concludes:

> In this story there is nothing that children may not know. Still, the children have *not* heard it. I have told it only to the dark, to no one else. And the children are afraid of the dark, and run away from it, and if some time they have to stay in it, they press their eyes shut and put their fingers in their ears. But for them also the time will come when they love the dark. From it they will learn my story, and then they will understand it better, too.[1]

The dark that the narrator refers to is the dark that surrounds his life, our lives, and all things. It is the darkness of our origins and the darkness of our destiny. The story he tells is a story of two old friends who meet again after many years and find themselves together waiting for a wonderful guest, who they know once was and who they sometimes think will be. The story is a story of God's absence, yet the absence in this instance is one that holds the promise of a presence yet to be. As a story told to the dark, it is a story that holds out hope, for it intimates that the dark need not be empty and those who find themselves in the dark need not be desolate.

3

Stories told to the dark, the stories we need to be "in the dark" to hear, are as numerous as the stars that steal from the night its terror and as various as the flashes of imagination that engender them. Like the stars, they make the present night of unknowing bearable; yet also like the stars they are without number. How can we find one among the many to guide us in the night?

In the pages that follow we will be exploring the infinite spaces of stories told to the dark, taking our bearings from different modes of imagining that can be discerned in them. Our task is like that of mapping the skies, determining the constellations. We set about our task in part to be at home in the dark, so that when our life draws near its close we may lay it down without fear; but also in part that we may recognize a star of extraordinary brilliance, a star that we, like the Magi, may follow in our lifetime.

It is my belief that, while stories are infinite in number, they tend to constellate in correspondence to certain modes of imagining. We will consider five such modes. The mode of imagining discerned in most myths we will call "innocent"; the mode of imagining prevalent in gnostic stories we will call "fallen"; that which is typically modern and the dominant mode of imagining in fiction we will call "alienated"; that which contains within it a critical component and which marks the writings of western mystics we will call "purged"; that which announces its presence in the *Divine Comedy* and hardly anywhere else we will call "sanctified."

The types I have proposed are not meant to be exhaustive. They should be regarded roughly as maps. Road maps are useful for finding the way from one place to another. Topographical maps are better for locating the heights and depths of the terrain. Inevitably the decision to be guided by a particular map has the effect of eliminating prospects that the mapmaker did not think to incorporate. The particular map I am offering, implicit in the modes of imagining I have proposed and in the order in which I have presented them, lends itself best to a Dante-esque journey into hell, up a seven-storied mountain, to a region where will and desire are moved by the love that moves the sun and the other stars. From dark wood to Light that powers the stars, from stories told to the dark to the radiant source of all our imaginings— Dante's journey is our own.

CHAPTER 1

Shadows

Innocent Imagination: Sing Songs,
Shadows Realities

"You ask me to dig in the earth? Am I to take a knife
and plunge it into the breast of my mother? But then, when
I die, she will not gather me again into her bosom. You tell
me to dig up and take away the stones. Must I mutilate her
flesh so as to get at her bones? Then I can never again enter
into her body and be born again. You ask me to cut the
grass and the corn and sell them, to get rich like the white
man. But how dare I crop the hair of my mother?"[1]

These words, spoken by a Sioux Indian, Smohalla, less than
a century ago, belong properly in a story told to the dark. Though
we no longer have that story, we can surmise that it would tell how
the first people lived for awhile in the womb of the earth before
emerging into the light of day. They dared not violate their
mother, for they knew the day would come when they must return to her womb. Their hopes for new life, for rebirth, are inextricably linked to the preservation of their inviolate relation to the
land. No wonder they resisted the white man's attempt to accul-
turate them, to make of them a farming people.

7

To someone on the outside of such a story looking in, its accents may be strange, its vision an illusion, the projection of a merely subjective meaning. The story might well be called mythical. Yet the Greek word for myth, $\mu\nu\theta$, meaning quite simply story or tale, did not originally connote falsehood. Myth did not stand in a subordinate relation to science, as if it were some prescientific, fabulous account for what was later to be better described in scientific terms. "Myth" gathered these relatively negative connotations only when the stories of the Greeks became the preoccupation of strangers who, not being *in* the stories, could only relate to them as quaint, archaic, fabulous tales. For someone who is *in* the story, however, as Smohalla seems to be in the story of his tribe, there is nothing false, illusory, quaint, or fabulous about it. His story fulfills what the historian of religion, Mircea Eliade, takes to be the original function of myth: it lays bare the structure of the world and makes clear to its adherents how to locate themselves within that world.[2]

Although it is risky to generalize about the function of myth even in the way Eliade has, it is possible to discern in stories like Smohalla's the operation of imagination in a distinct mode. While a particular myth might display more a social, political, or psychological function, the "innocent" imagination that produces it invariably serves the needs of someone who is *in* the story. I can illustrate what I mean by telling a story about a story.

One day my three-year-old daughter Rachel and I were sitting in our living room, a room that is notable only for an enormous pillow that takes up a disproportionate amount of space in the middle of the floor and that Rachel used as an indoor gym throughout a very long winter. I decided to tell her a story about a pillow, a very large pillow, that lived in the middle of the forest. The pillow was a very happy pillow, because every day all the animals in the forest would come and frolic on it. At the end of the day, when the animals went to bed, the pillow would go up to the sky and sleep with the clouds. Well, one night there was a big wind that blew the pillow and all the clouds away; so when the animals came the next morning, the pillow was gone. At this point I was about to bring my little story to a close, saying that the animals all got together and made a pillow to remember their friend by and to frolic on. Before I had the chance, however, Rachel interjected instead, "And here it is, in our living room!"

The point of this story is not to suggest that the innocent imagination is childish or that myths are only for children or primitives. What is important is that Rachel was in a real sense *in* the story she ended, and I was not quite *in* the story I began. Rachel's story virtually overflowed from the pillow itself. Something that big and fluffy which was already so many things to Rachel begged to be celebrated in story, just as anything marvelous moves us to speech, to express our wonder about what it means. The meanings we each attached to the pillow, my rather artificial meaning and her quite natural and spontaneous meaning, derived in part from our quite different experiences. She brought to the story hours of pillow-frolicking and her memories of multitudes of stories about animals in forests. I brought to it hours of delight in her pillow-frolicking, memories of stories about animals in forests, and memories of all the ways theologians try to fathom the mysteries of the Christian faith. Rachel, in jumping right into the story (jumping in so completely that she could end it), taught me how I *should* have ended the story I began if I were really *in* it. Her conclusion was true to the reality of the pillow. The flaw in the story I intended to tell was that the pillow was forgotten at the last moment for the sake of a not very profound or sound theological point.

If there is a real substantial core to myth—if myth is not after all simply illusion, the flimsy projection of subjective meaning—it is because at its wellsprings is a thing that really is or an event that really happened (and continues to happen) which gathered meanings as someone first told and others continued to tell stories about it. It is not that the stories *invest* the event or thing with meaning. The meaning is there in abundance, awaiting and, in some instances, compelling recognition. Eliade sometimes speaks of myth as the world's speech. He means, I think, that the things of the world and the events of the life have an excess of meaning, part of which the storyteller attempts to register. The world "breaks into speech" when the storyteller channels the overflow.[3] What matters is that the storyteller is moved to speech by something that strikes him as marvelous.

When we speak, then, of innocent imagination, we refer to the kind of imagining that celebrates what is marvelous. It does not attempt to offer an explanation that would exhaust something's meaning, as "fallen" imagination is inclined to do. Rather its story engages a person more fully and richly in the experience of the thing itself. Rachel's story about the pillow served to increase her delight in frolicking on it perhaps in part because through the story she learned that the kind of delight she took was an essential ingredient of the pillow—her spontaneous response to it "fit."

Although products of "innocent imagination" may appear in any age, the most conspicuous examples are to be found in antiquity. In the pages that follow we will first consider a story that celebrates the birth of civilization: the Babylonian creation epic, *Enuma Elish*. We will then turn to the story of creation affirmed by the composer of *Genesis*. Both stories exhibit imagination in its innocent mode, and a consideration of *Genesis* shows that the affirmation of the story told to the dark by innocent imagination is anything but childish. From this brief study we will realize that we, too, may be in a story. It may be a story we know, as it was for the composer of *Genesis*, or it may be a story we have yet to hear. As a story told to the dark, it is a story we appreciate most when we are grown up.

*   *   *

The *Enuma Elish* opens with the following account of the birth of the gods:

When above the heaven had not (yet) been named,
(And) below the earth had not (yet) been called by a name;
(When) Apsu primeval, their begetter,
Mummu, (and) Tiamat, she who gave birth to them all,
(Still) mingled their waters together,
And no pasture land had been formed (and) not (even)
     a reed marsh was to be seen;
When none of the (other) gods had been brought into being,
(When) they had not (yet) been called by (their) name(s)
    and (their) destinies had not
    (yet) been fixed,
(At that time) were the gods created within them.[4]

In rapid succession there come into being Lahmu and Lahamu, Anshar and Kishar, Anshar's firstborn Anu, and finally Anu's offspring, Ea, who is "broad of understanding, wise, mighty in strength, much stronger than his grandfather, Anshar."[5] The younger divinities make such a din that Apsu cries out to Tiamat:

"Their way has become painful to me,
By day I cannot rest, by night I cannot sleep;
I will destroy (them) and put an end to their way,
That silence be established, and then let us sleep!"[6]

Tiamat is horrified:

"Their way is indeed very painful, but let us take it
    good humoredly!"[7]

Mummu, however, offers Apsu encouragement, and Apsu most assuredly would have killed them had not Ea become aware of his designs. Ea charms Apsu to sleep with a holy incantation. He takes from Apsu his royal tiara and his supernatural radiance. Then he slays Apsu and imprisons Mummu. After thus vanquishing his foes, Ea retires to his abode, takes Damkina for his wife, and begets Marduk, mightiest of the gods.

    Tiamat meanwhile is incited to avenge the death of Apsu. She confers upon her new spouse, Kingu, the tablet of destinies and prepares to join battle with her offspring. Once again Ea becomes aware of the plot, but this time he is numb with fear. He knows that the incantation that had charmed Apsu to sleep will not suffice in the confrontation with Tiamat. He realizes that all the might of Marduk will be required to withstand Tiamat's onslaught. So Ea calls Marduk to his room and reveals his plan. He encourages Marduk to stand before Anshar.

Marduk goes to Anshar and strikes a hard bargain:

> "If I am indeed to be your avenger,
> To vanquish Tiamat and to keep you alive,
> Convene the assembly and proclaim my lot supreme."[8]

Anshar then convenes the gods, who solemnly decree:

> "Marduk, thou art our avenger:
> To thee we have given kingship over the totality of the
>   whole universe."[9]

To show his power to make good his word, Marduk with a simple command first destroys and then restores a garment brought before him. The gods rejoice, and Marduk goes forth to challenge Tiamat to single combat:

> She became like one in a frenzy (and) lost her reason.
> . . . The lord spread out his net and enmeshed her;
> The evil wind, following after, he let loose in her face.
> When Tiamat opened her mouth to devour him,
> He drove in the evil wind, in order that (she should) not (be
>   able) to close her lips.
> The raging winds filled her belly;
> Her belly became distended, and she opened wide her
>   mouth.
> He shot off an arrow, and it tore her interior;
> It cut through her inward parts, it split (her) heart.
> When he had subdued her, he destroyed her life;
> He cast down her carcass (and) stood upon it.[10]

After slaying Tiamat and imprisoning the gods who aided her, Marduk binds Kingu and takes from him the tablet of destinies. He returns to Tiamat, splits her into two parts, and with half of her forms the sky as a roof to hold back her waters. He then creates stations for the gods, determines the constellations and the calendar, and reveals to Ea his plan for the creation of man:

> "Blood will I form and cause bone to be;
> Then will I set up *lullu*, 'Man' shall be his name!"[11]

Ea counsels Marduk to alter his plan and to deliver up a brother of the gods from which to fashion man. Marduk accedes. He assembles the great gods and Ea, with the blood of the scapegoat Kingu, creates mankind. He sets free the captive gods and imposes their services upon mankind. The gods wish to make a sanctuary for Marduk to express their gratitude. Marduk, visibly pleased, says:

> "So shall Babylon be, whose construction ye have desired;
> Let its brick work be fashioned, and call (it) a sanctuary."[12]

So it is that they build a temple for Marduk in which to take up his abode.

The rest of the story is comprised of a recitation of the fifty names of Marduk. These names are to be remembered and handed down from generation to generation so that man's land may be fruitful and that it may be well with him.

There can be no question that the hero of this story is Marduk and that the story is essentially the story of those who honor him. To tell that story, the storyteller reaches back to a time that not only precedes Marduk but also precedes naming. From an undifferentiated beginning there springs into being a procession of deities, each generation more powerful than the last. With each generation there also comes more turbulence, until at last Apsu's patience is exhausted and he decides to destroy his own offspring.

If every father had his way, the human race may have died out long ago; at least, this is the humorous suggestion of the storyteller who has struck upon a wonderfully simple analogy close to every man's home to "shadow" the turbulence of precivilized life.

In this story Ea, notable for his wisdom and understanding (and also for the strength of his magic), soothes Apsu with his words, puts him to sleep, relieves him of his power, and slays him.[13]

However, the storyteller seems convinced that more than wisdom and understanding are required for a society that will endure, for Tiamat remains to stir up the kind of violence that is so well imaged in the storm. In the storm, Nature's visage is uncaring, senseless, violent beyond human measure. Ea's magic will not check Tiamat. Tiamat will be mastered only by one whose might is greater and, in this story at least, by one who secures the benediction of the gods gathered in solemn assembly. Marduk, blessed by the gods, shows even before engaging Tiamat in single combat that he has the power to make good his word when, before the gods, he causes the garment to disappear and to appear again.[14]

The significance of the slaying of Tiamat, the dramatic climax of the story, can hardly be overstated. With her death, the whole host of supernatural powers aligned with her are disarmed and obliged to render service to Marduk. Marduk creates the cosmos from the body of Tiamat. To each god he assigns a station. The very conditions for civilized life are thus established. In this sense, the birth of civilization coincides with the death of Tiamat. The storyteller's wonder is aroused by that event lost in the past when men no longer lived at the mercy of Nature but managed to subdue her. His story does not *explain* the beginning of civilization; it rather brings that event to the fore so that it may be properly celebrated.

The rest of the story is the story of man as much as it is the story of Marduk. Man is created from the blood of Kingu to render service to Marduk. Mankind, whose blood came from a divinity wed to Tiamat—whose nature, presumably, is as wild and brutal and violent as hers—is now subject to Marduk. His life belongs to Marduk and, in serving him, he incidentally maintains the order of the cosmos that Marduk established. The fact that each of Marduk's fifty names is related to a distinct human activity suggests that so long as his names are remembered and honored, so long as his people live every facet of their lives in his name, Marduk's power to sustain the cosmos and the state will endure.

We know now that the *Enuma Elish* was annually recited by the high priest before the statue of Marduk in the course of the New Year's celebration in Babylon. In fact, it is quite possible that parts of it were dramatized, the king playing the role of Marduk, the priests taking the parts of the other gods. As the story tells the story of Marduk's exaltation, so presumably its ritual reenactment would have had for its purpose the confirmation of the supremacy of the Babylonian king ruling in Marduk's name.

Yet to see the *Enuma Elish* only in terms of its historical-political-liturgical significance is to ignore the features we have referred to that contribute to its mythic density. Doubtlessly the event the *Enuma Elish* celebrates is the rise of Babylon to political preeminence. But that event, as it is presented in this story, has a meaning far more profound than would be obtained in any ordinary historical narration. The emergence of, and the continued ascendancy of, Babylon is an awesome event to the imagination that tells this story. The existence of Babylon means that Tiamat's day has passed, that a fully human life is possible. It is, then, not so much the emergence of Babylon to political supremacy that interests the storyteller as it is the emergence of civilized man from out of subjection to the uncaring, brutal, and senseless forces of Nature. It is this deeper tone that sounds in the *Enuma Elish*, enabling it to transcend the historical confines of a merely regional story.

Finally, we note that the storyteller has no interest in *explaining* the rise of Babylon by locating that event within the sweep of an inevitable historical process or within the interplay of forces that the gnostic alone could comprehend. His story awakens in his listeners a sense of the significance of the event that *is* Babylon; it would involve them more fully and richly *in* it. This unwillingness to exhaustively explain something is discernible in most myths and is related to the involvement of the storyteller in what his story is about.

Gabriel Marcel makes a similar point in *The Mystery of Being*.[15] Inasmuch as persons are inevitably part of the being they inquire about, they cannot obtain the objectivity that seems to attend scientific inquiry and to enable technicians to "solve problems." Where the subject is inescapably involved in the object of inquiry, there is no longer a problem to be solved or something to be comprehensively explained but a mystery to be fathomed. It is as if depths are necessarily fathomed by someone who has entered into them rather than by someone secure on the surface.

Jacques Maritain, too, catches something of the involvement of the storyteller in his story when he writes:

> . . . the *metaphysical* myths are the organic signs and symbols of some faith actually lived, be it by the primitive man; they are forms (either properly mythological or genuinely religious) through which a conviction of the entire soul nourishes and quickens from within the very power of creative imagination. Such myths have no force except through the faith man has in them.[16]

The distinction Maritain offers here between "some faith actually lived" and faith's "organic signs and symbols" helps to sharpen the meaning of what it is to be in a story. We might say it is the "conviction of the entire soul" of the composer of the *Enuma Elish* that serving Babylon is his people's way of participating in the ordering of the cosmos, and that it is this conviction that "nourishes and quickens from within the very power of creative imagination" that gives birth to the story. In one sense the story is incidental; the creative imagination might have fired a thousand other stories. In another sense, however, the story is essential; to reject it or mock it would be to reject or mock the conviction it embodies. In this sense the composer is in his story. And the people to whom his story speaks are in the story too. It is not necessary to presume that the hearer takes the story to be literally true, though it seems that in any age there are those whose manner of being *in* the story is to take it literally. It is sufficient to suppose that the faith or conviction the story embodies is unshakeable.

When the particular faith or conviction is lacking, when a person or people are not involved in what a particular story celebrates, when they are not *in* that story, they will not insist on its truth. More likely will they assert the truth of another story that more fully embodies their faith. If they are a captive people, they may well incorporate echoes of the story of their captors in order to distinguish their own story's accents sharply from it. Quite possibly something like this happened while the Hebrew people were in captivity in Babylon between 587 and 530 B.C.

That there are striking resemblances between the *Genesis* account of creation and the *Enuma Elish* has been noted ever since the first fragments of the Babylonian story were discovered and collected in the middle of the nineteenth century. While some have gone so far as to suggest that the *Genesis* story is *founded* upon the earlier Babylonian account, it now seems more likely that the composer of *Genesis* meant to present an account that would preserve intact the identity of a captive people whose faith and convictions were quite different from that of the Babylonians. There are undeniably echoes of the *Enuma Elish* in *Genesis*. Whether or not we accept the suggestions that have been made regarding the common etymological derivation of the Babylonian *Tiamat* and the Hebrew *Tehom* ("the deep" in "and there was darkness over the deep") and the subsequent correspondence between the use of Tiamat's corpse to make the firmament and the separation of the waters for the same purpose in *Genesis*, we cannot ignore the fact that the order of creation in the two accounts is identical.

Yet more impressive than the points of contact in the two works are the divergences. *Genesis* 1-2:4 is silent about the birth and procession of the gods. Furthermore, creation takes place by the power of a God who lacks all the anthropomorphic trappings of Marduk and whose word alone suffices to create everything— from nothing. Finally, the Creator makes man and woman in his own image, whereas, in the *Enuma Elish*, Ea makes man from the blood of a conquered (and presumably evil) deity.

If the account of creation in *Genesis* 1-2:4 which tells how the Lord created everything in six days and rested on the seventh is intended to clarify the precise departures of the Hebrew story from the Babylonian story, the inclusion of the older account of creation in *Genesis* 2:4-4 which tells about Adam and Eve suggests that the composer of *Genesis* wishes to remind his people of an ancient story of their own that more faithfully embodies their deepest convictions about their relation to God and their place in the world. That story begins:

> At the time when Yahweh God made earth and heaven there was as yet no wild bush on the earth nor had any wild plant yet sprung up, for Yahweh God had not sent rain on the earth, nor was there any man to till the soil. However, a flood was rising from the earth and watering all the surface of the soil. Yahweh God fashioned man of dust from the soil. Then he breathed into his nostrils a breath of life, and thus man became a living being.
>
> Yahweh God planted a garden in Eden which is in the east, and there he put the man he had fashioned. Yahweh God caused to spring up from the soil every kind of tree, enticing to look at and good to eat, with the tree of life and the tree of the knowledge of good and evil in the middle of the garden.[17]

As the story continues, the Lord God takes the man and puts him in the garden to till it. He tells the man he may eat of every tree in the garden—except of the tree of the knowledge of good and evil. To provide company for the man he created, the Lord makes the birds and beasts and brings them to man for him to name. Finally, the Lord puts the man to sleep and takes one of his ribs and from it makes woman. She is tempted by the serpent, subtlest of beasts, and eats the forbidden fruit. She then gives some to Adam, who also eats it. The Lord brings them to confess their deed, condemns the serpent, determines the punishments for Adam and Eve, and excludes them from the Garden lest they eat of the tree of life and live forever.

The person who first told this story was not interested in the birth of civilization, the ascendancy of Babylon or of any other nation. Evil and, in particular, the fact of death provoked this story. The composer of *Genesis*, the person or persons responsible for including the story of Adam and Eve, remained involved in a story that fostered no illusions about the conjunction of wisdom and might in the person of a king. His people were apparently far more impressed with a fault in the foundations of any political order, a fault for which they had no comprehensive explanation —just a story that encouraged them to ponder what they could not understand.

It has been observed that the story of Adam and Eve does not account for the origin of evil in terms of Adam's sin alone:

> . . . it speaks also of the adversary, the Serpent, who will become the devil, and of another personage, Eve, who represents the vis-à-vis of that Other, Serpent or Devil . . . and from those counterpoles it gets an enigmatic depth by which it communicated subterraneously with the other myths of evil . . .[18]

When asked in effect why he ate of the forbidden fruit, Adam replies, "It was the woman you put with me; she gave me the fruit and I ate it."[19] The woman in turn says, "The serpent tempted me and I ate."[20] Though there is no question that later theologians properly located "the fall" in *Adam's* transgression, it is just as clear that Adam's sin resists explanation. His pointing to the woman and her pointing to the serpent only serve to postpone the question and to locate it in a context where there are no answers forthcoming. The story does not put an end to the question about the origin of evil; it rather shows some of the question's ramifications and invites the listener to ponder what defies explanation. One of the best known reflections on the story, Augustine's account of his theft of some pears in his *Confessions*, only brings him to the same mysterious edge. The most that he can discern is that there was no *reason* for his act; it was absurd, irrational. Furthermore, it was an act he would never have done alone.

Actually, the *Genesis* story goes just a bit further than Augustine in suggesting some of the "reasons" Eve ate of the fruit: "you will be like gods, knowing good and evil"; "the tree was good to eat"; it was "pleasing to the eyes"; "it was desirable for the knowledge that it could give."[21] Still, the very multiplying of "reasons" which themselves only raise further questions does not stop our wonder but invites us to probe further into the mystery of evil. We are invited not to solve a problem, as if evil is a problem to be solved, but to fathom further and further a mystery that resists explanation.

While it is the deepest conviction of the Babylonian story-teller that service to Babylon is the way to participate in the creative ordering of the cosmos because in the Babylonian ruler might and wisdom are at last conjoined, the composer of *Genesis* finds himself in a story that has no illusions about the conjunction of wisdom and might in the person of a king. (Divine pretensions, after all, were among the "reasons" Eve ate of the forbidden fruit.) The stories are irreconcilably different, worlds apart. Yet they have in common a feature it would be possible to discover in other myths as well. Both are stories in which the storytellers are involved and which, therefore, they take absolutely seriously.

*   *   *

When myth is understood as an embodiment of an unshakeable faith, it is clearly not a category reserved for people in a distant past. We too may be in a story. To discover the story we are in, we might begin by finding our own statements comparable to Smohalla's. We will learn about that story as we lay bare the foundations of our convictions. Were we to tell the story that defines us, we would be relying on our power of imagination to blaze a path into the dark that surrounds our lives. Were someone else to tell us such a story, we would respond with enthusiasm because we would realize that it is our story. *That* story we would not regard as false, illusory, quaint, or fabulous because it would embody the faith we more obscurely live.

Though the myth is an embodiment of a faith or a conviction that fires the creative imagination, there is nowhere the implication that the myth is an adequate or complete expression of that faith. As with the *Enuma Elish* and *Genesis*, the climactic events tend to be the densest in terms of imagery and attendant meanings. For it is here that the composer is most involved. It is not that the composer is trying to be subtle or clever; it is quite otherwise. The story mirrors his own inexhaustible mystery at the same time it points to the event that inspires his awe. Innocent imagination, therefore, is content to "shadow forth" dazzling things. It is markedly different from the imagination that has no time or taste for shadows.

CHAPTER 2

Projections

Fallen Imagination: Constructs Explanations, Projects Illusions

In the years of Ardashir King of Persia I grew up and reached maturity. . . . The Living Paraclete . . . revealed to me the hidden mystery that was hidden from the worlds and the generations: the mystery of the Depth and the Height: he revealed to me the mystery of the conflict and the great war which the Darkness stirred up. He revealed to me how the Light (turned back? overcame?) the Darkness by their intermingling and how (in consequence) was set up this world . . . he enlightened me on the mystery of the forming of Adam the first man. He instructed me on the mystery of the Tree of Knowledge of which Adam ate, by which his eyes were made to see; the mystery of the Apostles who were sent out into the world to select the churches (i.e., to found the religions). *Thus was revealed to me by the Paraclete all that has been and that shall be, and all that the eye sees and the ear hears and the thought thinks.*[1]

We have been describing imagination in its innocent mode as the possession of someone who is *in* the story, in awe of some thing or happening that provokes an attempt to "shadow forth dazzling things." The storyteller has no pretensions about offering an all-encompassing explanation; he is content to remain among the shadows, pondering, taking to heart what has evoked his wonder.

The person who recorded the words cited above has no time or taste for shadows. He speaks of a revelation, an illumination, that leaves nothing, nothing at all, in the dark. "Thus was revealed to me by the Paraclete all that has been and that shall be, and all that the eye sees and the ear hears and the thought thinks."[2] It is the statement of a convert, one who has been literally turned around. A whole way of relating to things has passed away to be replaced by another.

We can apprehend more precisely what is involved in such a conversion by considering a parable from antiquity, Plato's parable of the cave. That parable begins:

> . . . Behold! human beings living in a sort of underground den, which has a mouth open towards the light and reaching all across the den; they have been here from their childhood, and have their legs and necks chained so that they cannot move, and can only see before them; for the chains are arranged in such a manner as to prevent them from turning round their heads. At a distance above and behind them the light of a fire is blazing, and between the fire and the prisoners there is a raised way; and you will see, if you look, a low wall built along the way, like the screen which marionette players have before them, over which they show the puppets . . .
>
> And do you see, I said, men passing along the wall carrying vessels, which appear over the wall; also figures of men and animals, made of wood and stone and various materials; and some of the passengers, as you would expect, are talking, and some of them are silent? . . .
>
> And they see only their own shadows, or the shadows of one another, which the fire throws on the opposite wall of the cave? . . .
>
> And of the objects which are being carried in like manner they would only see the shadows? . . .
>
> There can be no question, I said, that the truth would be to them just nothing but the shadows of the images.[3]

Plato then invites his listener to imagine a course of events set in motion when one of the prisoners is released and compelled to turn around. First he sees the figures passing over the bridge, the imitations of things existing outside the cave. Finally he is dragged into the light of day where at last things are seen as they really are.

The mode of imagining we are calling "fallen" is the characteristic mode for the gnostic storyteller who has fallen out of an innocent, direct relation to things and events, but who has not made the journey out of the cave. He has turned away from a more immediate relation to things and happenings in favor of a relation to things hidden from the view of simpler souls. These things he takes to be the underlying reality for what passes before the eyes of those who have not been turned around. The one who has been converted, turned around, sees the things being carried across the bridge (though not the carriers), and his gnosis consists of an apprehension of the relation of the shadows to these objects. The intelligent act here as elsewhere is that of seizing upon a significant relationship, of making connections insightfully. The reason for considering the act of imagining in this mode fallen is in part because the storyteller has fallen from a kind of simplicity; but the primary reason we assign a term with negative connotation to this mode is that the person whose imaginings are situated within the perspective of the "freed prisoner" is sadly mistaken in his judgment that he has discovered the ultimate truth about the shadows that are the fare of simpler souls. He is freed only in the sense that he will never mistake the shadows for realities, which is the characteristic pitfall for the naive. But the gnostic is not free in that he has not discerned that what he faces now are fabrications, imitations of things existing outside the cave. In relating the shadows to the fabrications and in mistaking the fabrications for the real, the gnostic is like someone attempting to define the reality of a table in terms of its atomic structure, forgetting that that atomic structure is an imaginative construct and not the ultimate explanation of the table. When he elevates the imaginative construct to "the really real," he is in fact projecting an inner reality (for the imaginative construct, be it atomic structure, electromagnetic field, ether, or whatever, originates *within* intelligence) onto a world of objects. If the simpler soul faces shadows, if his imagination "shadows forth" dazzling things, the gnostic beholds a world of projections, mistaking his projections for revelations. He believes he has been given a revelation. It does not occur to him that in fact he has been constructing an explanation. If the simpler soul must resist the temptation to insist dogmatically upon the ultimate reality of shadows, the gnostic is susceptible to a dogmatism far more dangerous because what he projects as truth has its origin in a subject that has not and cannot be critically scrutinized. The gnostic simply does not perceive the artificiality of what he takes to be the hidden reality.

Because the gnostic is unwilling to abide shadows, the revelations he affirms tend to be comprehensive explanations that promise to illumine absolutely everything. "Thus was revealed to me by the Paraclete all that has been and will be, and all that the eye sees and the ear hears and the thought thinks."[4] None of life's enigmas remain for this spirit. Moreover, because the enigmas can be explained, stories about enigmas can be corrected. If the myth tends to leave things in shadow because the storyteller has not been enlightened, the gnosis will disclose how the myth *should* have been told.

Examples of the kind of mentality I have been describing are numerous in modern times. We need only consider the syntheses of Marx and of Freud to discover that the mode of imagining which we will be more exhaustively portraying in gnostic stories continues to flourish.

In Marx's early writing, in his *Critique of Political Economy*, we are struck by the attempt to make sense of history. While the simpler soul faces "one damn thing after another" and, at best, becomes accomplished in recognizing certain patterns and predicting a likely course of events, Marx is not content until he has discovered the underlying forces that determine the entire course of human history. In the passage that follows, we can see a bold attempt to reduce the problem of understanding the entire panoply of historical events to that of grasping certain economic forces that determine political and social structures and constitute therefore the *meaning* of historical events:

> In the social production which men carry on they enter into definite relations that are indispensable and independent of their will; these relations of production correspond to a definite stage of development of their material powers of production. The sum total of these relations of production constitutes the economic structure of society—*the real foundation, on which rise legal and political superstructures and to which correspond definite forms of social consciousness. The mode of production in material life determines the general character of the social, political, and spiritual processes of life.* It is not the consciousness of men that determines their existence, but, on the contrary, their social existence determines their consciousness. At a certain stage of their development, the material forces of production in society come in conflict with the existing relations of production, or—what is but a legal expression for the same thing—with the property relations within which they had been at work before. From forms of development of the forces of production these relations turn into their fetters. Then comes the period of social revolution. With the change of the economic foundation the entire immense superstructure is more or less rapidly transformed.[5]

What Marx suggests here and elsewhere is that the shadowy course of human events can be illumined in terms of a comprehensive theory of economic forces and pressures. But that theory rarely receives critical scrutiny; it is rather dogmatically, almost religiously affirmed. The meaning Marx thinks he has found *in* history becomes the basis of a dream that held and continues to hold the minds and hearts of thousands of people.

The appeal of such a magnificent synthesis we can readily understand when we consider, for the moment, that one without a philosophy of history is inevitably faced with happenings that combine to make a collage of slaughter, injustice, and infamy that no sensitive soul can bear. Who would not, if he could, turn away from the photograph of the Vietcong prisoner being shot in the head in order to sweep that event and others like it into a scheme that could be understood and controlled—so that such events could never again occur to evoke our shame? Who would not accept the revelation of "all that has been and that shall be, and all that the eye sees and the ear hears and the thought thinks"[6]?

Freud's explanation of religion is, if anything, an even better example of the operation of fallen imagination. Consider the following passages from *The Future of an Illusion*:

> When the growing individual finds that he is destined to remain a child forever, that he can never do without protection against strange superior powers, he lends those powers the features belonging to the figure of his father; he creates for himself the gods whom he dreads, whom he seeks to propitiate, and whom he nevertheless entrusts with his own protection. Thus his longing for a father is a motive identical with his need for protection against the consequences of his human weakness.[7]

> . . . religious ideas . . ., which are given out as teachings, are not precipitates of experience or end-results of thinking: they are illusions, fulfillments of the oldest, strongest and most urgent wishes of mankind. The secret of their strength lies in the strength of those wishes.[8]

The testimony of a John Henry Newman or of a Gerard Manley Hopkins, to name only two, stands little chance of having a hearing in the court of psychoanalysis. What Newman writes in his *Grammar of Assent*, "If, as is the case, we feel responsibility, are ashamed, are frightened, at transgressing the voice of conscience, this implies that there is One to whom we are responsible, before whom we are ashamed, whose claims upon us we fear,"[9] Freud would wrench out of its context and situate within the psychoanalytic context, transforming the voice of conscience into the voice of the superego. In a manner faintly reminiscent of the way Ea charms Apsu to sleep, steals from him his power and so slays him, Freud charms the soul to sleep and a god dies.

By the time Hopkins writes "God's Grandeur," the sense of God's presence has diminished, but it is not as thin as Freud's bloodless rendering would have it. Hopkins expressed the feelings of many when he wrote:

> The world is charged with the grandeur of God.
>   It will flame out, like shining from shook foil;
>   It gathers to a greatness, like the ooze of oil
> Crushed. Why do men then now not reck his rod?
> Generations have trod, have trod, have trod;
>   And all is seared with trade; bleared, smeared with
>   toil;
>   And wears man's smudge and shares man's smell: the
>   soil
> Is bare now, nor can foot feel, being shod.
>
> And for all this, nature is never spent;
>   There lives the dearest freshness deep down
>   things;. . .[10]

In Newman and in Hopkins, the inner and the outer world remain theaters in which God is the principal actor. Spirits like their own can wander there and find assurance that their God lives. They do not delve for hidden meanings but testify to meaning's overflow. The kinds of experiences they describe are inevitably "decoded" by the Freudian, who has already decided that religious ideas are fulfillments of mankind's most urgent wishes. These very experiences can be exhaustively explained in terms of an economics of instincts; there is no need to resort to transcendent reasons. Hence the Freudian is less interested in the images of God than in understanding the set of needs projected in the images.

What it is important to note about both Marx and Freud (and, for that matter, about any ideologist) is that neither is content until he has constructed a comprehensive explanation for the phenomenon in question: of history, in Marx's instance; of religion in Freud's. Each is like the freed prisoner who has turned away from the shadows and who, with a powerful imaginative synthesis, has linked the shadows with the figures passing over the bridge. Each is convinced that he has discovered the underlying, fundamental reality, hidden from the view of the prisoner, that finally and definitively explains what passes before the eyes of simpler souls and deludes them. One who is attached to his imaginative synthesis with the compulsion of a convert cannot tolerate an alternative view. The insight that liberates suddenly fixes, freezing him in a rigid dogmatism from which release is difficult.

The examples of imagining in its fallen mode that we have considered from the modern period characteristically take the form of theories elevated to the status of laws rather than stories. No doubt the emergence of science in modern times has contributed to this development. It is, however, quite possible to discover products of fallen imagination much earlier in human history that display some of the same ideological features we have already noted. These early outpourings of imaginative activity are far more lavish in the use of figures than the more conceptual representatives of recent years. In the pages that follow, we will focus our attention on two stories from the first Christian centuries: "The Hymn of the Pearl" and the Manichaean story. We will begin in both instances with the text or a summary of the text. Before analyzing them further, we will suggest some of the reasons for the stories' special power. In the instance of "The Hymn of the Pearl," for example, we will recognize that part of its power is related to its genuine insight into a common human experience. Finally, however, we will indicate the manner in which the gnostic imagination remains frozen in a perspective whose limitations it is unable to grasp, for which reason we regard it as "fallen" imagination.

A. "THE HYMN OF THE PEARL" *(Text abridged as indicated)*

"When I was a little child and dwelt in the kingdom of my Father's house and delighted in the wealth and splendor of those who raised me, my parents sent me forth from the East, our homeland, with provisions for the journey. From the riches of our treasure-house they tied me a burden; great it was, yet light, so that I might carry it alone. . . . They took off from me the robe of glory which in their love they had made for me, and my purple mantle that was woven to conform exactly to my figure, and made a covenant with me, and wrote it in my heart that I might not forget it: 'When thou goest down into Egypt and bringest the One Pearl which lies in the middle of the sea which is encircled by the snorting serpent, thou shalt put on again thy robe of glory and thy mantle over it and with thy brother our next in rank be heir in our kingdom.'

"I left the East and took my way downwards, accompanied by two royal envoys, since the way was dangerous and hard and I was young for such a journey; I passed over the borders of Maishan, the gathering-place of the merchants of the East, and came into the land of Babel and entered within the walls of Sar-bug. I went down into Egypt, and my companions parted from me. I went straightway to the serpent and settled down close by his inn until he should slumber and sleep so that I might take the Pearl from him. Since I was one and kept to myself, I was a stranger to my fellow-dwellers in the inn. Yet saw I there one of my race, a fair and well-favored youth, the son of kings (lit. 'annointed ones'). He came and attached himself to me, and I made him my trusted familiar to whom I imparted my mission. I (he?) warned him (me?) against the Egyptians and the contact with the unclean ones. Yet I clothed myself in their garments, lest they suspect me as one coming from without to take the Pearl and arouse the serpent against me. But through some cause they marked that I was not their countryman, and they ingratiated themselves with me, and mixed me (drink) with their cunning, and gave me to taste of their meat; and I forgot that I was a king's son and served their king. I forgot the Pearl for which my parents had sent me. Through the heaviness of their nourishment I sank into deep slumber.

"All this that befell me, my parents marked, and they were grieved for me. It was proclaimed in our kingdom that all should come to our gates. And the kings and grandees of Parthia and all the nobles of the East wove a plan that I must not be left in Egypt. And they wrote a letter to me, and each of the great ones signed it with his name.

" 'From thy father the King of Kings, and from thy mother, mistress of the East, and from thy brother, our next in rank, unto thee, our son in Egypt, greeting. Awake and rise up out of thy sleep, and perceive the words of our letter. Remember that thou art a king's son: behold whom thou hast served in bondage. Be mindful of the Pearl, for whose sake thou hast departed into Egypt. Remember thy robe of glory, recall thy splendid mantle, that thou mayest put them on and deck thyself with them and thy name be read in the book of the heroes and thou become with thy brother, our deputy, heir in our kingdom.'

"Like a messenger was the letter that the King had sealed with his right hand against the evil ones, the children of Babel and the rebellious demons of Sarbug. It rose up in the form of an eagle, the king of all winged fowl, and flew until it alighted beside me and became wholly speech. At its voice and sound I awoke and arose from my sleep, took it up, kissed it, broke its seal, and read. Just as was written on my heart were the words of my letter to read. I remembered that I was a son of kings, and that my freeborn soul desired its own kind. I remembered the

Pearl for which I had been sent down to Egypt, and I began to enchant the terrible snorting serpent. I charmed it to sleep by naming over it my Father's name, the name of our next in rank, and that of my mother, the queen of the East. I seized the Pearl, and turned to repair home to my Father. Their filthy and impure garment I put off, and left it behind in their land, and directed my way that I might come to the light of our homeland, the East.

"My letter which had awakened me I found before me on my way; and as it had awakened me with its voice, so it guided me with its light that shone before me, and with its voice it encouraged my fear, and with its love it drew me on. I went forth. . . . My robe of glory which I had put off and my mantle which went over it, my parents . . . sent to meet me by their treasurers who were entrusted therewith. Its splendor I had forgotten, having left it as a child in my Father's house. As I now beheld the robe, it seemed to me suddenly to become a mirror-image of myself: myself entire I saw in it, and it entire I saw in myself, that we were two in separateness, and yet again one in the sameness of our forms. . . . And the image of the King of kings was depicted all over it. . . . I saw also quiver all over it the movements of the gnosis. I saw that it was about to speak, and perceived the sound of its songs which it murmured on its way down: 'I am that acted in the acts of him for whom I was brought up in my Father's house, and I perceived in myself how my stature grew in accordance with his labors.' And with its regal movements it pours itself wholly out to me, and from the hands of its bringers hastens that I may take it; and me too my love urged on to run towards it and took it and decked myself with the beauty of its colors. And I cast the royal mantle about my entire self. Clothed therein, I ascended to the gate of salutation and adoration. I bowed my head and adored the splendor of my Father who had sent it to me, whose commands I had fulfilled as he too had done what he promised. . . . He received me joyfully, and I was with him in his kingdom, and all his servants praised him with organ voice, that he had promised that I should journey to the court of the King of kings and having brought my Pearl should appear together with him."[11]

Comment:

One of the most remarkable things about this song, a gnostic piece found in the apocryphal Acts of the Apostle Thomas, is the occasion on which it is supposed to have been sung. The apostle Thomas had just been imprisoned in India and was rejoicing in his call to share in Christ's glory in the martyrdom he expected to endure. It is a song he sang in the face of death. Whereas the *Enuma Elish* and *Genesis* are stories of a particular people, the story that lies in the circle of this song has a universal appeal, striking a powerful chord in the heart of everyone who must someday die. "The journey into the deadlands to bring beauty back,"[12] here imaged in the son's journey into Egypt to bring back the one pearl, is a journey anyone of us might make.

Part of the song's power, however, rests in the fact that, while anyone might undertake the journey, very few of us even consider the possibility. People in every age fall into the routine of living each day as if they will live forever. We are wonderfully forgetful of the death that circles the life like a serpent, waiting to devour us. However, while in our conscious living we may for the greater part of our lives manage to ignore the fact of our own mortality, our moods witness to the uneasiness of submerged facets of our personalities in the face of a fate that cannot help but be felt as threatening. Part of the song's power, therefore, is related to its capacity to constellate many of our unformed feelings about death. Its principal images and motifs bring those feelings into sharp focus and open up the possibility of gaining insight into moods that are otherwise opaque to us. If the song did no more than that, it would be a remarkable song. In fact it promises even more. What constitutes its drama is its unraveling of the way the power of death to rule the life is broken. It promises nothing less than salvation from death to the person who lives in the circle of the song.

In "The Hymn of the Pearl" two ways of living are contrasted: that of the dwellers in the Eastern kingdom and that of the Egyptians. The life of the Egyptians, the life of the dead-lands,[13] is life passed in a drunken stupor, a kind of oblivion, a failure to acknowledge the monstrosity that encircles it. An immortal coming into contact with such a people might think they had been charmed or drugged into a deep sleep to live so mindlessly an existence circled on every side by death. There is, however, in the image of the inn circled by the serpent the hint that the underside of the strange denial of death is an unformed fear or dread, the sort of fear a slave has for a master.

The image of the encircling serpent can be further illumined by imagining for a moment an individual who is considering the course his life may take. He stands at the center of a circle. His possible lives are the various routes he might choose from the center to the perimeter—the infinite number of radii. He knows that any course he takes, any line he lives out, will come abruptly to an end. The one at the center, therefore, because he can consider his life as a whole from beginning to end, knows that any course he follows out from his center is a course that is bounded. All the possible lives terminate, and the line linking all the terminations is like the perimeter of a circle. That end might be subliminally *felt* as dreadful; then the serpent circling the life could become a powerful way to focus feelings that he has not hitherto engaged. The image becomes a way of coming into touch with his feelings.

What then becomes exciting about the story is that it tells how the power of the serpent to rule the life is broken, how the serpent is charmed to sleep and the one pearl is recovered. As the pearl is found in an ugly shell at the bottom of the sea, so, the storyteller suggests, the soul is found in a body that is sunk in life and awaits redemption. The story of that event is the story of an inner transformation. With that transformation the power of death to rule the life is broken.

The structure of "The Hymn of the Pearl" reinforces the storyteller's point about that transformation. The form of the story is circular. It begins and ends in the East. The son goes down into Egypt by way of Maishan, Babel, and Sarbug and returns by way of Sarbug, Babel, and Maishan. Before setting out he takes off his robe of glory. When he returns with the pearl he again dons the robe of glory which has grown precisely as he has grown in the course of his journey. Furthermore, within the circle of the song are a series of lesser circles. The entire song is like a series of chain links, whose last link is joined again to the first. Each event in the story both foreshadows the next and reminds us of the one that went before. The most dramatic instance of an event that looks both backward and forward is that of the message which takes the shape of an eagle. The message itself reminds us of the message originally inscribed on the heart and later inscribed in the letter. The message is a reminder, signalling that the time of forgetting is past. The message becomes wholly speech and awakens him; the time of sleep is past. The message is an eagle, a figure that reminds us of his kingly origin but which also foreshadows the end of the serpent's dominion, since the serpent is the natural prey of the eagle. The neutralization of the serpent's power to encircle and hold the life in its shadow, first announced in the arrival of the eagle, is again represented in a figure that looks back to the story's beginning and forward to the story's end. The son charms the serpent to sleep, reminding us of his original plan and of his own fall. The removal of the serpent as threat announces the recovery of the pearl, but that event simply foreshadows the exchange of his impure garment for his robe of glory and his exaltation.

All the attention to circles should make us realize that the song itself is a circle of circles. For one who lives in the circle of the song, the power of the serpent to hold the life in its shadow has been broken. *The encircling serpent is replaced by the circle of the song.* The song itself is meant to perform the same function for the one who hears it as the message did for the one who went down into the deadlands to bring beauty back. The song means to save him from a soulless, spiritless existence and to carry him beyond the narrow confines of a life dominated by death and its fear.

There is a child's story about God that neatly leads to a similar insight.[14] A man's life is like a line, it says, because it has a beginning and it has an end. God's life is like a circle, because it has no beginning and it has no end. A man hopes that when he comes to the end of his line he will find that his line ends—in a circle. The circle that is God's life is a hopeful circle, as hopeful as the circle of the song. True, one does not reach the circle before one reaches the end of the line. Flannery O'Connor quoting St. Cyril of Jerusalem writes:

> "We go to the Father of Souls, but it is necessary to pass by the dragon." No matter what form the dragon may take, it is of this mysterious passage past him, or into his jaws, that stories of any depth will always be concerned to tell, and this being the case, it requires considerable courage at any time, in any country, not to turn away from the storyteller.[15]

"The Hymn of the Pearl" does not spare us the experience of the serpent. It does, however, hold the promise of a wholeness that is won by facing up to the serpent wherever and whenever he would insinuate himself into our lives. Most profoundly this means recognizing that at the bottom of our moods is a grim denial of our own mortality. The song offers us a way of recognizing what is eating us and would devour us if we would let it; it has the effect of liberating us, offering the kind of freedom that salvation from death's power means.

Reservations:

The insight that wholeness depends upon our facing up to the serpent is valid and it is, indeed, liberating. That insight as expressed in the hymn, however, is inseparable from the context expressed in the song's dominant, though concealed, metaphor—the metaphor of exile. The story is, in fact, the metaphor of exile extended. In this song the way one can overcome the serpent is to remember that this world is not a home, was never meant to be one, and exists only so that one may discover one's true self and return to the father whose kingdom is not of this world. It is a vision a hair's breadth from Christian orthodoxy.[16]

We begin to notice in the concealed metaphor of exile the characteristic feature of fallen imagination, the deliberate turning away from the events and things of life in favor of a hidden truth in terms of which life's enigmas can be resolved. For the gnostic who composed the hymn, what is, on the face of it, a hospitable place—a kind of inn—is not what it appears. He insinuates that we are not at home in the world because we are in exile. Our true home is elsewhere. Once we grasp this hidden truth, we are in a position to comprehend life's enigmas. Even suffering and death make sense if they remind us of our true home.

As with any sufficiently encompassing image, there is something attractive and even compelling about the thought that the image of exile engenders. It makes sense of a considerable portion of human experience. But there is also something about the image that is treacherous, for it tends to screen out those experiences that challenge its claim to define the life. Life's joys must be felt as lures. If first the image liberates the one it "catches," it quickly freezes the spirit and holds it in the fastness of its particular vision. Moreover, because there is so very much at stake in affirming the story—it offers no less than a solution to the problem of death in its promise of a hidden wholeness and a future glory

—there is the real danger of being unable to see around the story, even as the ideologist is unable to break out of the confines of his particular theory.

The concealed metaphor of exile that pervades the narrative of "The Hymn of the Pearl" and provides the cipher for decoding human experience and for understanding "all that has been and that shall be, all that the eye sees and the ear hears and the thought thinks,"[17] is abundantly elaborated in the story of Mani, the third-century self-proclaimed prophet who regarded his teaching as the consummation of that of his three predecessors, Buddha, Zoroaster, and Jesus. That story shows graphically the extremes to which fallen imagination is prepared to go in order to preserve intact its own powerful synthesis. Although we do not have a text as reliable as that of "The Hymn of the Pearl," it is possible to reconstruct Mani's story from fragments that appear in Christian polemical writings and from scrolls discovered more recently. To that story we now turn.

B. THE STORY OF MANI: *Summary*

According to Mani, before heaven and earth came to be there were two principles, the one good and the other evil. The good principle, called the Father of Greatness, dwelt in the place of Light; the evil principle, called the King of Darkness, inhabited the land of Darkness. Though the world of Light bordered on the world of Darkness, there was no wall dividing them. The Light was satisfied with the separation and had no inclination to enlighten the Darkness. Hence their subsequent interaction was rooted in the nature of Darkness. The nature of Darkness was hate and strife, and, in the course of internal warfare, the Darkness reached its own outer limits. There it perceived the Light as an external and better object. Obsessed with a desire to mix with the Light, the Dark powers prepared to fight against it in order to subdue it.

In defence the Father of Greatness produced a series of cre-

ations culminating in a representation of his own self. This last
creation, "Primal Man," was charged with the struggle against
the Darkness. With his five sons, Primal Man plunged rapidly
from the heavens down to the border of Darkness. Their mission,
however, was quickly aborted. The Dark Lord surrounded Primal
Man and devoured his sons. Nonetheless, the devouring had its
effects on the devourer. The devoured Light acted like a soothing
poison, and the attack on the world of Light by the Dark powers
was stopped.

To free Primal Man, the Father of Greatness called forth a
second creation, the Living Spirit, who descended and extended to
Primal Man his right hand. Grasping it and ascending, Primal
Man became a god again, but he left behind the Light that had
been mixed with Darkness. For the sake of these lost parts the
cosmos was created as a great mechanism for the separation of the
Light.[18] In a final strategem to impede this process, the Dark
Lord produced Adam and Eve and poured into them all the Light
left at his disposal. To Eve he imparted concupiscence so that she
might seduce Adam; through their ensuing reproduction he
hoped to prolong indefinitely the captivity of the Light. Seeing
through the plan, the heavenly powers sent the "luminous" Jesus
to warn Adam. It was the luminous Jesus who made Adam eat
from the Tree of Knowledge so that he might understand his
predicament. Adam, however, was seduced in spite of the warning. His fall made necessary a history of revelation, through Buddha, Zoroaster, Jesus, and finally Mani, wherein the knowledge
that the luminous Jesus originally conveyed to Adam might be
made available throughout the ages. Life, then, for the Manichaean was seen as a struggle between powers of Light and
powers of Darkness and history was regarded as the continual
process of the freeing of the Light.[19]

Comment:

The story's power to gather together in brilliant synthesis

the movements of the heavens and the stirrings of the soul is a
startling and thrilling thing to perceive. Perhaps the nature of the
synthesis can be illumined by a story Marie Louise von Franz
once told of her conversation with a palm reader whose technique
she was trying to understand. This palm reader would normally
blacken the palm of his client with charcoal and then press it
down on a piece of paper. He would then "read" the imprint.
When she remarked, "You really knew all about the person as
soon as you met, didn't you?" he replied, "Of course—only I
could not have expressed it without referring to the imprint of the
palm." Von Franz's point was that the palm reader's knowledge
of the client was an unconscious knowledge. The process of divin-
ing, of bringing to consciousness what was unconsciously perceived, depended upon the mediation of the design of the imprint.
It served to constellate the unconscious apprehensions and to give
them expression. What the diviner had to learn was not something unknown about his client so much as something hidden
within himself, first activated by the client and later given expression in the image—in this instance, in the design left by the
blackened palm. Something analogous seems to be at work in
Mani's story, where the motions of the heavens provide an occasion or a medium for discovering truths of the soul.

    We repeat, then, that to the Manichaean, existence is in re-
ality a struggle between powers of Light and powers of Darkness.
That struggle becomes "visible" when it is projected onto the
cosmos. The configuration of the heavenly bodies becomes the
medium for revelations about the soul. In this way the astrolo-
gers' heavenly charts become maps of the inner life. Although the
story preserves intact the connection of inner and outer worlds, we
can penetrate it further by considering them separately.

    In Nature the struggle between the powers takes place every
day as the sun goes down or, in terms of the story, as Darkness
swallows the sinking sun and as Light is broken into the moon
and stars. While at first it seems that Darkness has overcome

Light, in fact the power of the moon and stars to diminish the terror of the night is the promise of the coming of a new dawn, when the sun will again show its face and renew the earth.

The corresponding inner drama is begun when dark, turbulent feelings threaten to engulf a person. The conscious self, the daytime self, ordinarily has no interest in exploring the dark; it is only when ego-consciousness feels itself about to be engulfed that it acts. In order to survive the onslaught one must find a way of engaging the feelings that threaten to overwhelm one. As the Father of Greatness is moved to a series of creations culminating in a *representation* of himself that goes forth to do battle, so one's imagination is activated and, in dream and fantasy, spins off the images, motifs, and stories that permit one to engage one's feelings. As Primal Man is rescued by the Living Spirit and restored to the Godhead, so one's dreams and fantasies may be fathomed and so illumine consciousness.

What is remarkable about the Manichaean story is that it holds together in brilliant synthesis what I have just taken apart. The inner relation between the movements of the heavens and the stirrings of the soul is magnificently caught in the story. But that inner relation is *constituted* by an imaginative act that finds in events recurring in Nature a divine drama, more than meets the eye of the simple soul. What the fallen imagination does not realize is that the drama it discovers is a drama it first brings. It is a drama of the soul that it projects upon the cosmos and takes as the underlying meaning in terms of which *everything* can be understood. Hence it is not content to have penetrated to the very core of events in Nature; it must be able to incorporate in its vision human acts as well.

The way Mani incorporates history is by suggesting that the struggle between the powers of Darkness and Light since Adam takes place in time. While the decisive event in the process has already taken place out of time in the struggle and exaltation of Primal Man, its perfection is nonetheless prolonged indefinitely until at some time lost in the future all the light shall return to its source. Within this theology of history, the meaning of God's revelations in Buddha, Zoroaster, and Jesus is perfectly clear. The knowledge that the luminous Jesus imparted to Adam and that became available historically through these prophets was finally and definitively proclaimed in the Manichaean story. While the course of human events might be obscure to simpler souls who face a wilderness of shadows, the Manichaean hearer possesses the cipher that illumines the dark, eliminates shadows, lays bare "all that has been and that shall be, and all that the eye sees and the ear hears and the thought thinks."[20]

Nor is that all-encompassing knowledge without its moral edge. It becomes essential, once the nature of the struggle is understood, that the individual descend into the darkness within, undergo something like death, and then respond to the call to greatness and identify with that spark of divinity within—say, with all one's noblest instincts—and in so doing become one with the process whereby light is restored to its source. The life to which the elect were called was one of strict asceticism. They despised marriage and sexual intercourse. They observed an uncommonly strict fast, eating only food that had been prepared by others, lest they be guilty of taking the life of any living thing. It was theirs to become perfect in this life so that the light within them might return at last to its source. If one found this regime too severe, one could yet serve those who were further along the way and hope in another incarnation to have a higher place in the economy of souls.

What probably sustained those who embraced the Manichaean story was the certitude that the decisive deed was eternally accomplished in the victory of Primal Man. That deed, moreover, could be witnessed daily in the sacrament of the universe. As the diviner knows the hidden truths of the soul in the medium he employs, so the convert could read the destiny of mankind in the skies. Mani's story provides a synthesis so startling and so compelling that he could almost be forgiven for thinking it divine.

Reservations:

As with any powerful synthesis, the danger is in being blinded by the light. One becomes blind to the experiences that challenge the synthesis and blind to its true origin. In order to preserve intact the vision, the adherent must play fast and loose with those facts of life that refuse to fall in line. The Manichaean story amply illustrates the extent to which fallen imagination is prepared to go to preserve its synthesis, as Augustine was among the first to perceive.

In his *Confessions*, Augustine looks back on the nine years he spent as a Manichaean aspirant with great bitterness. That one of Augustine's stature should be enthralled by the Manichaean revelation for nearly ten years is a powerful witness to the attraction of that story a century and a half after Mani's death. It may also explain why, in the *Confessions*, Augustine is so vehement in his rejection of Manichaeism. He is the first to expose the ways in which the avowal of the story did violence to what the eye sees, the ear hears, and the thought thinks.

His first objection to the Manichaeans, and perhaps in his age the most damaging, was that their story did not square very well with the findings of science. Augustine is speaking of the scientists of his time when he writes:

> All the same I remembered many of the true things that they had said about the created world, and I saw that their calculations were borne out by mathematics, the regular succession of the seasons and *the visible evidence of the stars*. I compared it all with the teaching of Manes, who had written a great deal on these subjects, all of it extremely incoherent. But in his writings I could find no reasonable explanation of the solstices and the equinoxes or of eclipses and similar phenomena such as I had read about in books written by secular scientists. Yet I was expected to believe what he had written, *although it was entirely at variance and out of*

*keeping with the principles of mathematics and the evidence
of my own eyes.*[21]

When we remember that the Manichaeans' hopes rested in
the decisive victory of Primal Man, the evidence for which was at
hand in the movements of the heavens, we begin to realize the
force of Augustine's first objection. For the Manichaean believer,
his objection would have occasioned a religious crisis comparable
to that suffered by Christian fundamentalists when paleontology
came into its own at the end of the nineteenth century.

Augustine's more serious objection to the Manichaean story,
however, was that it did violence to his own moral experience and
promised to mislead its followers precisely because it seriously
misconstrued the moral life. The force of his feelings can be felt
in the following renunciation:

> In Rome I did not part company with those would-be
> saints, who were such frauds both to themselves and to
> others. I associated not only with the aspirants, one of whom
> was my host during my illness and convalescence, but also
> with those whom they call the elect. I still thought that it is
> not we who sin but some other nature that sins within us. It
> flattered my pride to think that I incurred no guilt and,
> when I did wrong, not to confess it so that you might *bring
> healing to a soul that had sinned against you.* I preferred to
> excuse myself and blame this unknown thing which was in
> me but was not part of me. The truth, of course, was that it
> was all my own self, and my own impiety had divided me
> against myself. My sin was all the more incurable because I
> did not think myself a sinner. It was abominable wickedness
> to prefer to defeat your ends and lose my soul rather than
> submit to you and gain salvation.[22]

That Augustine named his autobiography *Confessions* perhaps indicates how seriously he objected to a story in which confession
had no place. That essential lack in the Manichaean story was
related to its fundamental claim about life as a struggle between
powers of Light and powers of Darkness. Far from offering a

solution to the problem of evil (as the dualism appears to do), the story prevents one from rightly considering the question. By supposing that in everyone there is some other nature that sins—something in one but not of one—the Manichaeans did violence to Augustine's moral experience. Readers of the *Confessions* who wonder why in his second book Augustine dwells so on what appears a trivial incident, his theft of a few pears, should notice there how frequently Augustine insists that it is he who did what he did. He may not be able to turn up any reasons, but that it was he who did it and he who was responsible for doing it—and he who must confess it—of these things he has no doubt whatsoever. To affirm the Manichaean story would compel Augustine to be blind to his own moral experience and lead him to misconstrue completely the nature of the moral life.

The last objection Augustine has must be inferred from the *Confessions*, since he nowhere states it. That objection is that Mani does violence to history when he subverts the *Genesis* story and produces a caricature of it with his interpretation. Mani apparently has so little regard for *Genesis* that he feels perfectly free to reverse the imagery. The Tree of Knowledge in the *Genesis* story is the tree from which Adam must not eat. In Mani's version, the luminous Jesus makes Adam eat of that tree. The characteristic feature of fallen imagination is nowhere more visible. It is not the straightforward narrative of *Genesis* that interests Mani, but the hidden meaning that brings to light all that is enigmatic in the narrative. That Augustine concludes his own autobiography with a commentary on *Genesis* suggests his concern to rectify in some measure the injustice of Mani's perversion of that narrative. It may also be that Augustine spends so much time dwelling on the theft of fruit to suggest that the Manichaean teaching, in which the eating of the fruit of the Tree of Knowledge is valued at the expense of the evident meaning of the *Genesis* story, is also a kind of theft. The Manichaean way of reading moral experience, in which evil is perpetrated by an other

nature in one but not of one, repeats a pattern evident in the
Genesis narrative when Adam shifts the responsibility for his
violation to Eve and Eve shifts it to the serpent. Augustine, in affirming the literal meaning of the *Genesis* account, may well have
meant to suggest that Mani's theft of that story is consistent with
Mani's moral teaching—and with Adam's and Eve's reprehen-
sible self-deception.

The inclination to distort experiences that do not fit snugly
into the imaginative synthesis, so easy to document in the Manichaean instance, is an inclination that can be discovered wherever
fallen imagination is at work. In its desire to leave nothing at all
in the dark, it artificially illumines everything. Yet it remains in
the dark about the actual origin of its synthesis. It fails to notice
that what it takes to be the hidden reality, the key to life's enigmas, is a fabrication. In mistaking its own fabrication for the real,
it is involved in projection of something within onto something
else. As the fabrication is but a rigid replica of something vital, so
the imagination that stands in awe of it is rigid, frozen in a
perspective from which it is difficult to be freed. It can neither see
around its synthesis, its story, nor does it see beneath it to its
roots, its source. It inhabits, therefore, a world of projections. It
has not discovered what Augustine suggests when he writes, "I
had my back to the light and my face was turned toward the
things which it illumined, so that *my eyes, by which I saw the
things which stood in the light, were themselves in darkness.*[23]
The move to interiority that this remark signals is the hallmark of
modernity. It marks a crucial advance in the movement of the
human spirit and leads to the production of a completely different
kind of story. The story of that development takes us into a consideration of alienated imagination.

CHAPTER 3

Mirrors

Alienated Imagination: Contrives Fictions, Fashions Mirrors

In the funhouse mirror-room you can't see yourself go on forever, because no matter how you stand, your head gets in the way. Even if you had a glass periscope, the image of your eye would cover up the thing you really wanted to see.

....

He died telling stories to himself in the dark; years later, when that vast unsuspected area of the funhouse came to light, the first expedition found his skeleton in one of its labyrinthine corridors and mistook it for part of the entertainment. He died of starvation telling himself stories in the dark . . .[1]

At this point in our journey it might be wise to take our bearings again in terms of Plato's cave analogy.

Imagination in its innocent mode tells stories, sings songs, about something marvelous or awesome right before its eyes. The innocent imagination does not attempt to deliver a comprehensive explanation because it is personally involved in what it is attempting to fathom. It has itself entered into the depths of something

47

finally mysterious. It is content, therefore, to celebrate what it takes to be an awesome fact and labors to awaken others to its significance. Its strivings are embodied in the shadowy figures and stories it fashions.

Imagination in its fallen mode tends to construct explanations. It is unwilling to live without a comprehensive vision of an underlying reality in terms of which to understand things that an innocent imagination finds awesome and prefers to leave in shadow. It does not so much celebrate awesome facts as it first projects and then discovers meanings it takes to be more fundamental. It fails to notice its own activity in constructing the synthesis with which it is so impressed and so tends to become frozen in its new perspective. Though it often recommends itself as consciousness raising, it simply replaces a naive dogmatism with another dogmatism that is more subtle and more dangerous.

In approaching imagination in its alienated mode, imagination in the modern context, we need to discover what transpired within the human spirit between the time of the ancients and the time of the moderns. Most notably we need to recall the advances in science which signalled a shift in the human spirit; then we need to consider the salient features of the philosophies that emerged to account for those advances. The point is not that alienated imagination was a product of modern philosophy. Rather, precisely because modern philosophers attempted to account for scientific advances in which imagination played a central role, they forged a particularly useful language and conceptual framework with which to display imagination in a new role. Accordingly, we will begin by isolating the pertinent developments in science and in philosophy that will enable us to better understand the imagination that gave birth to the novel. Then we will consider some of the works of two twentieth-century writers, D. H. Lawrence and John Barth. These two figures, as well as many others we might have chosen, display the predicament of the storyteller whose imagination is alienated.

A. From Copernicus to the Post-Hegelians

It is generally acknowledged that the ancients from the time of Aristotle considered the earth to be the stable center of revolving spheres. This view corresponded, after all, rather well to everyone's experience of the sun traversing the sky from east to west. Why should anyone think otherwise? Yet it is also well known that, in his famous publication of 1543, Copernicus proposed another way of seeing things in order to better account for the movements of the planets. He proposed that the sun be considered to be at the center and that the earth and other planets orbit the sun. Copernicus was, in effect, saying that things are not as they appear. We need to learn to look at things differently.

What has become for moderns the commonsense knowledge of planetary motion was far from obvious to people at the time of Copernicus. Certainly no one felt the earth moving, and it was perfectly clear that the sun rose and set. While many people were getting adjusted to a completely different way of understanding the relationship of earth and sun, a German philosopher was trying to understand what had made this particular scientific advance and a host of others like it possible. Immanuel Kant pointed out toward the end of the eighteenth century that unless Copernicus had said, "Suppose we understand the sun to be the center, suppose we organize our perceptions another way . . ." nothing very revolutionary would have occurred. What impressed Kant was the activity of Copernicus' imagination in the formulation of a completely different hypothesis. The great discoveries of Galileo and Newton afforded further glimpses of the power of supposing, which depended on a vigorous imagination. Oddly, before Kant, the key to the whole movement into modernity had not been noticed, or, if it had been noticed, it had not been clearly articulated. The act of supposing or imagining, whose philosophic import was not even perceived by Newton, caught Kant's attention; it led him to offer along similar lines a completely different hypothesis about the relationship of knowing to being, of the mind to the real. It is Kant's hypothesis that provides the conceptual frame for grasping the alienation of imagination that marks modern literature.

In German philosophy prior to Kant, the activity of the mind in the organization of perceptions was by and large unnoticed. It was thought that, just as our perceptions were faithful reproductions of real things happening in front of our faces, so our conceptions were faithful reproductions of the underlying structure of our perceptions. Our minds were regarded as passive reflectors of the real world. We think the way we do because the world is the way it is.

The only problem with this way of looking at knowing is that it misses the move Copernicus made (the move that has been made in every one of the sciences since then) when he said, "Suppose that, imagine that . . ." Even though Newton's own scientific advances depended upon following the lead of Copernicus, he too seems to have missed the import of his own act of supposing. His search for an Absolute Space—an absolute frame of reference —shows that his understanding of his own intelligent operation lagged behind his own scientific practice. He apparently still thought that his mind, when operating well, simply reflected like a mirror the objective structure of the real world. Hence he sought an objective, absolute space. Similarly, when he found the universe running like a clock, he thought of a divine clockmaker. It did not occur to him that clocks are human inventions. He still failed to grasp the import of the activity of imagination in the construction of the scientific hypothesis. In this sense, Newton's imagination was fallen.

Kant simply saw what Newton and others missed, and his superior observation produced a revolution in philosophy. He proposed to follow the example of Copernicus, only now in regard to the philosophical problem of the relation of the mind to the world. In his preface to the second edition of *The Critique of Pure Reason*, Kant wrote:

> The examples of mathematics and natural science, which by a simple and sudden revolution have become what they are now, seem to me sufficiently remarkable to suggest our considering what may have been the essential features in the changed point of view by which they have so greatly benefited. Their success should incline us, at least by way of experiment, to imitate their procedure. . . . Hitherto it has been assumed that all our knowledge must conform to objects. But all attempts to extend our knowledge of objects by establishing something in regard to them *a priori*, by means of concepts, have, on this assumption, ended in failure. We must therefore make trial whether we may not have more success in the tasks of metaphysics, if we suppose objects must conform to our knowledge. . . . We should then be proceeding precisely on the lines of Copernicus' primary hypothesis.[2]

In directing attention to the "essential features in the changed point of view" by which mathematics and the natural sciences greatly benefited, Kant located a shift in the human spirit of which the great scientific advances were but symptoms. In proposing that metaphysicians *suppose* that objects must conform to our knowledge, Kant was indeed following the lead of Copernicus and others whose work revolutionized natural science; but he was also proposing a way of understanding knowing that, while it was perfectly in keeping with the *practice* of the sciences of his day, marked a dramatic advance beyond the *thinking* of the very people who revolutionized science. The effect of Kant's proposal on the philosophic world was every bit as revolutionary.

In order to carry out a philosophic program built on the supposition that objects must conform to our knowledge, Kant needed to persuade people of the presence of two factors in any act of knowing: the forms of perception and the categories of thought.

The forms of perception, *space* and *time*, were the conditions of possibility for the organization of sensations into perceptions. In other words, if organizing intelligence did not operate always and everywhere with the benefit of these internal ordering principles, sensations would not be ordered as they are—extended in space and perduring through time. Because of necessity sensations are ordered according to the internal rules of the forms of perception, things are perceived as extended "in" space and "through" time.[3]

The categories of thought were similar to the forms of perception. These categories, like *substance, cause and effect*, and so on, were for Kant the conditions of possibility for the organization of perceptions into conceptions. If the organizing intelligence operated without the categories of thought, scientific knowledge would be impossible. Unless things were considered in terms of "substance," "cause," "effect," and so on, there would be no way to set up problems and, consequently, no way to know anything empirically. Because of necessity perceptions are ordered according to the internal rules of the categories of thought, things are thought of as substances, causes, effects, and so on. We can ask what "causes" something and obtain an answer that we can trust.

Kant insisted further that when science proceeds according to the regulations of the forms of perception and the categories of thought, its conclusions are universally and necessarily valid— absolutely reliable. Someone who understands his own intelligent operation, who knows how he has put together what he knows, can be certain that his conclusions are valid. We can now begin to appreciate Kant's significance for our exploration of imagination. In showing both *that* the person puts together what he knows and *how* he puts things together, Kant went beyond the point in the cave reached by fallen imagination. He recognized that what fallen imagination took for the real basis of something present in ordinary experience was but an artificial human product. In other words, whereas Newton thought his grasp of the marvelous order of the universe all but showed the existence of

God-the-watchmaker, Kant in effect said that watches are, after all, human artifacts. The order we discover is an order we impose. By supposing that the world explored by the empirical sciences is ordered according to universal and necessary principles of reason and so known, Kant thought that he could account for and provide philosophical warrant for the remarkable scientific advances of his day.

Nonetheless, Kant had to pay a considerable price for his philosophic gains. When asked *what* the scientist knows when he knows with certainty, Kant was forced to make a very important distinction between *phenomena* (that which shows itself under the conditions of human knowing) and *noumena* (things themselves, quite apart from any relation to a knower). Phenomena that appear in space and time lend themselves to empirical analysis and can be exhaustively known. About the noumena, however, absolutely nothing can be known. For this reason Kant could not prove but had to postulate noumena.[4] The distinction for Kant was not a distinction between appearance and reality because he was convinced that phenomena could be explained exhaustively in accordance with rules of reason that were universal and necessary. The scientist qua scientist had no interest in noumena. What mattered to him was that which showed itself under analyzable conditions and could therefore be empirically known. While the scientist could take comfort in the certitude of his conclusions regarding phenomena, not a few others were alarmed because there could be no comparable certitude about God, self, and world because, as Kant was the first to admit, God, self, and world were not phenomena.

If Kant could take comfort in the claim that God's existence could be neither proved nor disproved empirically, those who came after Kant were more inclined to lament with Nietzsche:

> But how have we done this? How were we able to drink up the sea? Who gave us the sponge to wipe away the entire horizon? *What did we do when we unchained this earth from*

its sun? Where is earth moving now? Where are we moving?
Forth from all suns? Are we not plunging unceasingly?
Backward, sideward, forward, everywhich way? Is there still
an above and a below? Are we not wandering through an
infinite void? Doesn't the empty space breathe upon us?
Has it not become colder? Is not night and more night coming perpetually? . . . The holiest and most powerful being
the world has hitherto known has bled to death under our
knives.[5]

The visible universe no longer offered intimations of its Creator
but merely reflected the ingenuity of the human imagination—a
feature of the modern consciousness that Kant did not, after all,
produce but simply diagnosed. Nietzsche's question, "What did
we do when we unchained this earth from its sun?"[6] poignantly
expressed the plight of the man who stood utterly cut off from a
transcendent source of meaning. "What was holiest and most
powerful of all that the world has yet owned has bled to death
under our knives."[7]

   The fate of the self after Kant is an interesting story. The
self to which Kant referred was not reducible to the self that appears. Insofar as we behave, enter into the time and space world
of an observer, others can construct laws that will serve well to
predict our behavior. The more unthinkingly we act, the more
our behavior will conform to those laws. Kant, however, postulat-
ed a self that eludes scientific analysis, a moral agent who, in not
appearing, is free. This is the self we know, as it were, from the
inside out though we cannot prove its existence empirically.

   What Kant held in a kind of dramatic tension did not long
survive. Positivists who denied the validity of anything that did
not lend itself to empirical analysis were not satisfied with Kant's
argument in the *Critique of Practical Reason*, his postulate of
freedom, or his moral self. At the other extreme, existentialists
who insisted on the priority of the freedom of the person, of the
"hole" in nature's fabric, of the "gap" in an otherwise continuous

line, resisted positivistic attempts to classify or chart human behavior. For Sartre, the being of humankind was *neantization*,
negativity. To be human was to bear negativity into the world, to
not-be anything he might be named. The only alternative to
being labeled and tabled, dissected and interred, it seemed, was to
be utterly nameless and lost, "straying through an infinite nothing."[8]

While the most dramatic consequences of Kant's distinction
between phenomena and noumena were the problematic status of
God and self, the most revolutionary development signalled by his
philosophy was the loss of an immediate, straightforward relation
to the things and events of life. Those who shared Kant's philosophic position could never again be simply in a story. While for
Kant it was a consolation to be able to ground science on the universal and necessary ordering principles deduced transcendentally,
those who came after him were far less sanguine than Kant about
the universality and necessity of the categories he deduced.

One of the first philosophers to challenge Kant on this
score, the philosopher whose response to Kant has been in many
ways the paradigm, was George William Friedrich Hegel. Hegel
represented Kant's crucial distinction of phenomena and noumena
in terms of an impenetrable curtain. In his chapter "Understanding" in *The Phenomenology of Mind*, he wrote:

> It is apparent that, behind the so called curtain which is
> supposed to conceal the inner reality, there is nothing to be
> seen if we do not go behind there ourselves, as much in order
> to see as that there may be something behind there that can
> be seen. But at the same time it is clear that we cannot without
> considerable pain go straight behind there; for this knowl-
> edge, which is the truth with respect to the understanding of
> the appearance and of its inner reality, comes only as a result
> of a laborious process . . . .[9]

The problem with Kant's analysis of knowing, from Hegel's point
of view, was that it short-circuited a *process* that was complete

only in the moment in which the self knows itself-knowing-an-*other*. Kant apparently regarded knowing as complete in the insightful synthesis, an essentially timeless, static event, as exemplified in the magnificent syntheses of classical physics (Galileo's, Newton's, and others'). Closer to home, the insightful synthesis happens the moment we have succeeded in making a connection, when we say "I've got it!" What Kant sought to uncover were the conditions for any synthesis, the necessary and universal ordering principles without which knowing would not occur. Had Kant paid attention to what he was *doing* instead of, or in addition to, what he was analyzing, he would have noticed that his "transcendental deduction" of the categories was his way of showing how the synthesis occurred. Before he completed his transcendental deduction, he did not know how he put things together in the insightful synthesis. But—and this is Hegel's point—knowing is not complete until the self has put things together *and* understood how it put things together—and when it has done that, *there is nothing more to understand.* What Kant missed, in Hegel's view, was the *act* whereby he deduced the categories. In the act of deducing the categories, Kant was in effect moving behind the curtain, becoming possessed of a self-knowing-an-*other*. He need not have posited noumena.

For Hegel, then, knowing is a process that includes logically three moments. The first moment is a moment of original union, in which knower and known are not differentiated. The knower is, as it were, lost in the other, as one might be lost in reverie or in a daydream. There is no self-consciousness at all. The second moment is a moment of alienation, in which the knower is attentive and is set over against an other that he attempts to approach with his special ways of ordering. One who has been interrupted in reverie and begins to pay attention can relate to his reverie from a reflective distance, refer to it as a "daydream" or with some other metaphor. This is the moment of observation *par excellence*, in which there are subjects and objects, when things-for-a-knower are laid out for dissection and analysis. It is the scientific moment, when the animate world in which one is involved withers away and suddenly becomes an object for an autopsy. It is the moment when the self of an other (or oneself, if one is considering oneself introspectively) becomes rigid, frozen in a particular classification. It is the moment when the divine dies under the knife. In order to know, Hegel submits, there needs be this perilous and profane moment when the other is objectified, rendered into a kind of corpse for dissection and analysis. No wonder Kant protested that some things are not fit subjects for empirical analysis!

Yet for Hegel this second moment of alienation is but one necessary moment in the knowing process. Unless objects are differentiated from subjects, *objective* knowledge would be a pipe dream. The other must be objectified if it is to be taken apart and put back together; and, in science, this is the kind of knowledge that counts. In this moment of alienation, the subject *must* diminish so that the object in its otherness may appear.[10] Hegel no less than Kant insisted upon the self-discipline that so characterized the new science. By insisting on this second moment, Hegel meant to incorporate in his philosophy all that Kant had gained.

But Hegel went beyond Kant when he insisted upon a third moment, a moment of self-appropriation in which the knower appropriates, makes the other his own. This moment involves, on the one hand, the fully conscious acceptance of the categories one relies on in approaching the other. On the other hand, it involves a grasp of the *other* in terms of those categories. The movement in which the other that has been objectified and laid out for analysis is made one's own resembles bringing the dead to life, to one's own life. One no longer merely plugs in formulas or follows recipes one does not understand, but rather one advances confidently to conclusions fully possessed of the capacity to derive the very formulas or recipes one is using. Hegel saw no need to exempt the world, the self, and God from scientific scrutiny. He was prepared to submit them all to the knife of analysis in the confidence that they might thereby live again in a self that had advanced from the cave, the womb, the tomb into the light of full knowledge.

Ironically, while Hegel intended to incorporate within his philosophy all that Kant had gained, he opened the way to a philosophic relativism that was the last thing either of them intended. When Hegel challenged the Kantian distinction of phenomena and noumena, affirming instead a third moment in which the knower, in full possession of the rules governing knowing, advances to knowledge of the other, he drew attention to the temporality of the act whereby Kant had deduced the categories. Kierkegaard's question, "Is an historical point of departure possible for an eternal consciousness?"[11] though it reaches much further in the direction of a religious point, suggests the direction in which philosophy went after Hegel. Those who followed after Hegel recognized and accepted Kant's claims that the world is necessarily a mediated world, a world already and always preordained in accord with regulations of reason; but they repudiated the notion that those regulations were universal and necessary. Far more likely it seemed that they were historically conditioned. The repercussions were dramatic. Kant had already rendered problematic the possibility of being *in* a story, be it mythical or gnostic. If we are, as Kant claims, persons who necessarily orient things in time and space in accordance with the categories of thought, the world before us is necessarily a mediated world, a world already precast according to our stipulations. We cannot simply be *in* the world but must ever peer into it through a lens that brings it into focus. When the universality and necessity of Kant's categories are challenged, one's relation to the world is rendered yet more problematic. The "world" before which one stands is a "world" one might compose in any number of ways. In other words, the modern alienated imagination knows that its products are its own creations, fabrications that serve as lenses with which to bring things into focus. Not only are the lenses infinitely various, but they reveal as much, if not more, about those who use them as they reveal about the world. The lenses are more mirrors than proper lenses.

If there were no movement beyond the moment of alienation, if one were in the position of forever trying out yet another lens, then one would be in a labyrinth of mirrors. Even so the prisoner in Plato's cave analogy who has had his head turned by philosophy and beholds the fabrications passing over the bridge in the firelight—and who recognizes them as fabrications—is in a quandary. In the firelight, it seems to him that the shadows are to be accounted for in terms of those human projections of which he has lately become aware. At this point in his journey it is not at all clear that the fabrications bear any resemblance to things as they really are. If he must live out his days in the firelight, if he beholds only things he has himself put together, the cave has indeed become a labyrinth of mirrors.

We have already observed that Hegel thought one might live *through* the moment of alienation. If his philosophy were construed as a kind of mirror, he would insist that it was like Alice in Wonderland's mirror. He could pass through it on his journey beyond the labyrinth. Hegel would have preferred another image for the cave, however, than that of labyrinth of mirrors. Rather would he have regarded it as womb-tomb, a place where, in the objectifying moment of alienation the world, the self, and the divinity were buried, yet a place from which there emerged new life as the self emerged into the light of full knowledge possessed of a new world, a new self, and a new God.

Others who came after Hegel regarded his philosophy as an illusion, his mirror as just another mirror in the labyrinth of mirrors.

    In the funhouse mirror-room you can't see yourself go on forever, because no matter how you stand, your head gets in the way. Even if you had a glass periscope, the image of your eye would cover up the thing you really wanted to see.[12]

For those who concur with Jean Paul Sartre that there is "no exit," the moment of alienation is not only the modern's point of departure. It is also the point to which he forever returns. It circumscribes his life and defines his condition.

Fiction writers after Kant and Hegel can be distinguished according to whether or not their fiction is meant to function as a mirror through which to pass out of the labyrinth or as but another mirror with which to make sense of things in the firelight. In either case they offer lenses or mirrors, artistic fabrications, contrived fictions. Their stories are marked with the kind of self-consciousness that distinguishes them from the stories of both innocent and fallen imagination.

In the first instance, the fiction writer is convinced, as was Hegel, that one can live *through* the moment of alienation. His fiction is a mirror that opens onto an imaginative space within which to objectify and resolve very real problems. The great advantage in focussing our attention on D. H. Lawrence's *The Rainbow* and *The Man Who Died* is that the very real problem reflected in them is the twentieth-century experience of alienation. Precisely by setting himself apart from that experience by reflecting it is his fiction, he was able to see deeply into the roots of the problem and to show how it might be lived through—by following the lead of his fictional characters.

More recent fiction writers seem not to cherish such hopes for their fiction. For them alienation is a problem that is not so easily lived through. They are inclined to think that there is no exit, but then, like John Barth, they remind us that, after all, it is a "fun" house we are lost in. They are content to do no more—and no less—than illumine yet another corner of the cave. Their fiction also reveals an intensification of their sense of alienation. Some write stories about writers writing stories, indicating a degree of self-consciousness that could only regard stories like Lawrence's which pretend to move through the dilemma as pretentious anachronisms. The dilemma—and the delight—of the storyteller at this dread pass is nowhere better displayed than in John Barth's *Lost in the Funhouse*. The dilemma: If there is no exit, why journey? If one would be fabricating but another mirror, why tell stories? The delight: It's fun to stumble through this place. Why not live a little? It's even more fun to delight one another with our distortions of the experiences. Why not tell stories? If you can't avoid alienation, at least you can make the most of it.

If the course of twentieth-century fiction can be illumined against the background of the course of philosophy after Kant, if we are now in a position to recognize the distinguishing features of the alienated imagination, it remains to attend to the stories of Lawrence and Barth to discover there the heights and the depths of stories told to the dark by alienated imagination.

B.   D. H. LAWRENCE

If Kant first explored the theoretical implications of the shift in the human spirit that made modern science possible, D. H. Lawrence was among the first to live in the world that science and technology produced. It is one thing to wonder theoretically or to fantasize about living in worlds that we are responsible for organizing; it is quite another thing to live in the world of concrete, machines, factories, pollution, and the brutalized form of work called labor. In this latter world, the loss of God, self, and world is not a theoretical loss but a real one. The imagination confronted with this kind of world does not have illusions about returning to a simpler, innocent, paradisiacal situation. The fiction writer cannot escape the predicament that defines his point of departure. Nor has Lawrence any intention of offering a fictional escape to a place of innocence. He begins with not just the idea of the loss of God, self, and world, but with the experience of that loss, and he imaginatively works *through* that loss in his fiction to a recovery of God, self, and world. But the experience of spiritual rebirth that he goes on to celebrate involves hammering out a new covenant. The world is a new world, the self a new self, the God a new God.

In the pages that follow, we will be focussing on two of Lawrence's works, *The Rainbow* and *The Man Who Died. The Rainbow*, one of Lawrence's early novels, shows Lawrence grappling artistically with the real problems of spiritual alienation that were felt in his world. By the time he writes *The Man Who Died* he is in full possession of his theme; in fact, he is almost dogmatic in his control of the narrative. In this respect, *The Man Who Died* is the distillation and crystallization of *The Rainbow*.

The Rainbow begins:

> The Brangwens had lived for generations on the Marsh Farm, in the meadows where the Erewash twisted sluggishly through alder trees, separating Derbyshire from Nottinghamshire. Two miles away, a church-tower stood on a hill, the houses of the little country town climbing assiduously up to it. Whenever one of the Brangwens in the fields lifted his head from his work, he saw the church-tower at Ilkeston in the empty sky. So that as he turned again to the horizontal land, he was aware of something standing above him and beyond him in the distance.[13]

We have here not only a precise description of the English countryside, but also Lawrence's witness to the absence of God in the exquisite figure of the church-tower *in the empty sky*. In one sentence Lawrence has caught the *experience* of the loss of God. There is no self-conscious wondering about the existence of God. That would be a theoretical problem. An empty sky connects not with an idea but with feelings, with experiences that are felt.

It takes him a little longer to mirror the alienation of the Brangwens from their world. At first the Brangwens were at one with the land. Indeed, it would be hard to find in literature a

more powerful portrait of that oneness than the following passage:

> They felt the rush of the sap in spring, they knew the
> wave which cannot halt, but every year throws forward the
> seed to begetting and, falling back, leaves the young-born on
> the earth. They knew the intercourse between heaven and
> earth, sunshine drawn into the breast and bowels, the rain
> sucked up in the daytime, nakedness that comes under the
> wind in autumn, showing the birds nests no longer worth
> hiding. Their life and interrelations were such; feeling the
> pulse and body of the soil, that opened to their furrow for
> the grain, and became smooth and supple after their plough-
> ing, and clung to their feet with a weight that pulled like
> desire, lying hard and unresponsive when the crops were to
> be shorn away. . . . They took the udder of the cows, the
> cows yielded milk and pulse against the hands of the men,
> the pulse of the blood of the teats of the cows beat into the
> pulse of the hands of the men.[14]

Blood-intimacy with the land, however, was not the only thing
the Brangwens knew. Their women "looked out from the heated,
blind intercourse of farm life, to the spoken world beyond."[15]
The world mediated by language, the "far off world of cities and
governments . . . where men moved dominant and creative, having turned their back on the pulsing heat of creation, and with
this behind them, were set out to discover what was beyond, to
enlarge their own scope and range and freedom,"[16] attracted the
women of the Brangwens long before the far-off world came
near. But the knack of speaking and the knack of making go
hand in hand. One day we carve out a world in speech; the next
day we slice the land with canals and railroads. It is the building
of a canal across the meadows of the Marsh Farm that made the
Brangwens "strangers in their own place. . . . Then the shrill
whistle of the trains re-echoed through the heart, with fearsome
pleasure, announcing the far-off come near and imminent."[17]

It has taken Lawrence but one sentence to bear witness to

the absence of God in the life reflected by his novel and seven pages to depict men's alienation from the natural world. He devotes nearly five hundred pages to the problem that most sorely grieves him throughout his life, the typically modern problem of self-alienation. He fastens his attention on relationships that feel the full force of the modern problem of self-alienation, relationships that are formed in the midst of that problem and grow strong in the course of living through that problem. Because Lawrence's deepest hopes lie in relationships of men and women, we are led to explore with Lawrence their fragile attempts to abide the tensions at the heart of human life.

The first part of the novel is a gentle tale of the "birth" of Tom Brangwen and the "rebirth" of Lydia Lensky. When first Tom and Lydia meet, the reader is informed that "there was an inner reality, a logic of the soul, which connected her with him."[18] That subtle connection is to be discovered in their different pasts.

Tom had always lived on the Marsh Farm between Cossethay and Ilkeston and was master of it from the time his father was killed in an accident. He worked and rode and drove to market. He went out occasionally with his friends for drinks, skittles, and little travelling theatres. The borders of his life were narrowly drawn, without hint of anything beyond Cossethay and Ilkeston. Until the time when he was seduced by a prostitute, he knew only one kind of woman—that represented by his mother and by his sister. That episode "put a mistrust into his heart, and emphasized his fear of what was within himself."[19] He became aware that "he had something to lose which he was afraid of losing, which he was not even sure of possessing."[20] For the first time he began to wonder whether he finally belonged to the world of Cossethay and Ilkeston. Thereafter Tom is consistently presented as one who is light, full of life in appearance, yet who harbors within him an unknown, a darkness that he fears to explore yet which he must somehow possess if he is to become whole. Lydia becomes the way for Tom to come to grips with the unknown within; she becomes the promise of his own completion, the end of an unreal, fragmentary existence.

Lydia was the daughter of a Polish landowner. When very young she married an intellectual, a physician whose political idealism and extreme patriotism led eventually to their emigration to London, where they became almost beggars. When he died soon after, Lydia was left with the care of their daughter Anna. For a long time Lydia "was like one walking in the Underworld, where the shades throng intelligibly but have no connection with one."[21] When she and Anna moved to Cossethay, her heart was stirred by the yellow jasmine and the persistent ringing of thrushes from the shrubbery: "she knew she was beaten, and from fear of darkness turned to fear of light."[22] Tom becomes for Lydia a promise of new life, and something buried deep within her is kindled by him: "she would wake in the morning one day and feel her blood running, feel herself lying open like a flower unsheathed in the sun, insistent and potent with demand. . . . She felt . . . the life in him."[23]

So Lawrence portrays the inner logic of their relationship. Each needs the other to be real, to move beyond their initial state of self-alienation. Yet each needs the other in a different way. Tom needs Lydia in order to possess what is unknown within him. Yet to give himself to his own depths is to run the risk of drowning, and the fear of the unknown never leaves him. Lydia, on the other hand, needs Tom as the flower needs the sun, to spring to life. Yet she feels that to expose herself to his light would be to be consumed by his flame.

Although there is a logic of the soul connecting Tom and Lydia, their coming together is not simple, nor is it a lasting thing as Lawrence portrays it. It is rather like a rainbow—something graced, transient, almost illusory, yet the token of a covenant more profound and more enduring. Both must overcome their complementary fears; both must resist complementary temptations. Tom must overcome his fear of the darkness, of the deep, of the unknown within him that attracts him to Lydia. He must resist the temptation to identify with Lydia the unknown that he needs in order to be whole. To look to her for his own wholeness would be to force her to become a goddess with whom to unite and thereby become immortal. To force her to be his completion would be to deny her her own reality, to annihilate her. No wonder she experiences his approach as that of a consuming fire that threatens to annihilate her. It is clear she would not survive the kind of union Tom is rushing into. Lydia, on the other hand, must overcome her fear of light, of the life in her that runs deeper than death. She must resist the temptation to identify the source of her life with Tom, to invest him with a divine power she needs to overcome the death in her. To force him to be her life source would be to reject his own reality, to drain life from him like a leach. No wonder he experiences her as one who threatens to devour him.

Their first encounters falter as they force each other to assume the roles of gods with whom they would unite in order to escape the human condition. They need to grow, to become more self-possessed. And so they do. Lydia becomes with child and becomes more and more unaware of Tom as she becomes more possessed of herself. At first her indifference makes him

> feel like a broken arch thrust sickenly out from support. For her response was gone, he thrust at nothing. And he remained himself, he saved himself from crashing down into nothingness, from being squandered into fragments, by sheer tension, sheer backward resistance.[24]

Little by little Tom learns "the bitter lesson, to abate himself, to take less than he wanted."[25] She, after all, "could only want him in her own way, and to her own measure."[26] He must find other centers of living, other centers of love, other selves to arch out to. First her daughter, Anna Lensky, receives part of his stream of life, and then other men. Little by little he becomes possessed of himself, and Lydia no longer feels the pressure of his need. When after two years of marriage they again embrace, Tom, who fears the unknown as much as ever, "let go his hold on himself, he relinquished himself, and knew the subterranean force of his desire to come to her, to be with her, to mingle with her, losing himself to find her, to find himself in her."[27] In letting Lydia be other—and in no other way—Tom becomes possessed of himself. Lawrence's first portrait of the way alienation—the experience of the absolute otherness of the other—is something like a death one endures in order to live is almost finished now. Lawrence needs no paraphrase. His last touch to this part of the novel says it all:

> Their coming together now . . . was the entry into another circle of existence, it was the baptism to another life, it was the complete confirmation. . . . Everything was lost, and everything was found. The new world was discovered. . . . They had passed through the doorway into the further space. . . . She was the doorway to him, he to her. At last they had thrown open the doors, each to the other, and had stood in the doorways facing each other, whilst the light flooded out from behind on to each of their faces, it was the transfiguration, glorification, the admission. . . . God . . . had passed through the married pair without fully making Himself known to them.
>
> Now He was declared to Brangwen and to Lydia Brangwen as they stood together. When at last they had joined hands, the house was finished, and the Lord took up his abode . . . .
>
> . . . Anna . . . was no longer called upon to uphold with her childish might the broken end of the arch. Her father and mother now met to the span of the heavens, and she, the child, was free to play in the space beneath, between.[28]

Tom and Lydia had to learn to accept each other's individuality. But to do that was to be thrown back upon their own limitations, limitations they could not expect an *other* to erase. When they finally reach out, each to the *other*, across the distance that both separates them and allows them to meet as equals, their reach becomes like the threshhold of a well-built house. The space they make is space in which their children are free to play and free to grow. Their reach that forms the threshhold that spans the heavens is also the sign of God's promise that he remains with them though everything pass away. Like the rainbow, such moments among men and women are fragile, transient, rare, experienced as a grace. When Tom is later carried away by the flood when the canal breaks down, as when he let go himself in loving Lydia, the reader does not feel regret. The reader's response is tempered by Lydia's:

> He had made himself immortal in his knowledge with her. So she had taken her place here, in life, and in immortality. For he had taken his knowledge of her into death, so that she had her place in death. "In my father's house are many mansions."[29]

In the second part of the novel, Lawrence returns to the same problem of self-alienation but from a slightly different angle. In this part Will is the dark figure, Anna the light. The two meet when Will, son of Tom Brangwen's elder brother, comes to live in Ilkeston. Anna is attracted to her cousin, who reminds her of a mysterious animal that lives in the darkness and never ventures out. He is like one who has been walking blindly through the darkness of infinite space, wondering where at the end of all the darkness God was to be discovered.[30] His very strangeness offers her release from her own narrow world. In this part of *The Rainbow*, however, Lawrence is more interested in exploring what Anna means to Will. He is dazzled by her. She moves like the moon through the darkness of his heart. He follows Anna like a shadow. When she says, "I love you, Will, I love you," he trembles with fear:

. . . he dared not think of her face, of her eyes which shone, and of her strange, transfigured face. The hand of the Hidden Almighty, burning bright, had thrust out of the darkness and gripped him. He went on subject and in fear, his heart gripped and burning from the touch.[31]

Her face, radiant with love, breaks into a region deep within him that had never been touched before. Yet the source of her radiance, like the sun in relation to the moon, remains hidden. She is at once moon moving through the darkness of his heart, the sun's dim reflection, and his touch with the bright hand of the Hidden Almighty. He gives flesh to his feelings, to his experience of her touch, in a woodcut, the Creation of Eve:

It was a panel in low relief, for a church. Adam lay alseep as if suffering, and God, a dim, large figure, stooped towards him, stretching forth His unveiled hand; and Eve, a small, vivid, naked female shape, was issuing like a flame towards the hand of God, from the torn side of Adam.[32]

We no sooner absorb this image than Lawrence superimposes another, like a photographer who superimposes two negatives. At either end of the woodcut are two angels covering their faces with their wings:

They were like trees. As he went to the Marsh, in the twilight, he felt that the Angels, with covered faces, were standing back as he went by.[33]

It is as if he is walking right into his own woodcut. In the passage that follows, the two are gathering together sheaves of corn in the moonlight, he coming, she going, he in darkness, her face in moonglow. In this second superimposed image, they undulate like waves drawn by the moon or like lovers approaching union:

They worked together, coming and going, in a rhythm, which carried their feet and their bodies in tune. She

stooped, she lifted the burden of sheaves, she turned her face
to the dimness where he was, and went with her burden over
the stubble. She hesitated, set down her sheaves, there was a
swish and hiss of mingling oats, he was drawing near, and
she must turn again. And there was the flaring moon laying
bare her bosom again, making her ebb and drift like a
wave.[34]

The close association of Anna with the moon becomes one of
identity in a passage that follows soon after, when Will embraces
her:

All the night in his arms, darkness and shine, he possessed of it all! All the night for him now to unfold, to venture within, all the mystery to be entered . . .
"My love!" she called, in a low voice, from afar. The
sound seemed to call him from far off, under the moon, to
him who was unaware.[35]

In part the image suggests that she is the occasion for him to
possess, to bring to light, his own darkness. But there is more. It
is as if he, drawn to her as to the moon, is drawn *through* her to
the dark nether side of the moon, which is perhaps again that
inner reality, the "logic of the soul which connected her with
him."[36]

The two images, that of the woodcarving and that of the
night scene, are practically superimposed. Corresponding to the
dark Adam is the darkness of the night sky—and Will. Eve, issuing like a flame towards the hand of God, corresponds to the
moon—and Anna. The dim large deity, like the sun whose rays
(hand) touch the moon, is the hidden source of light and power.
The two images provide Lawrence with the means of exposing
complementary temptations from which men and women need to
be freed if they are to resolve the fundamental problem of alienation. The temptation of the man is first imaged in the woodcarving, but later explained by Lawrence. Will, he writes, was ridden

by an awful sense of his own limitation. "It was as if he ended uncompleted, as yet uncreated on the darkness, and he wanted her to come and liberate him into the whole."[37] Will's temptation is to find in Anna the extension of himself, to subject her to his own requirements of wholeness. She is to be the Eve of his creation, part of his masterpiece, whose business it is to worship him. He seems not to notice how the dark figure of Adam and the Hidden Almighty are becoming fused. Anna, predictably, resists:

> "You've made Adam as big as a God, and Eve like a doll."
> "It is impudence to say that Woman was made out of Man's body," she continued, "when every man is born of woman. What impudence men have, what arrogance!"[38]

The temptation of Anna is evident in her reply, "every man is born of woman,"[39] and further illumined in an earlier passage:

> As time went on, she began to realize more and more that he did not alter, that he was something dark, alien to herself. She had thought him just the bright reflex of herself. As the weeks and months went by she realized that he was a dark opposite to her, that they were opposites, not complements.[40]

Anna's temptation is to think that Will is her bright reflex, as if she were the source of his life, vitality, and glory, more sun than moon. For a long time she fails to see that he responds not to something that belongs to her but to something far more powerful, of which she is but a dim reflection. The worship she expects and desires he is reserving.

Both Will and Anna must have their illusions shattered if they are ever to strike the kind of covenant that marks the marriage of Tom and Lydia. In this part of the story, Lawrence focuses his attention more on Will's progress than on Anna's. On their honeymoon, all is well with the deities:

It was as if the heavens had fallen, and he were sitting with her among the ruins, in a new world. . . . Here at the center the great wheel was motionless, centered upon itself. Here was a poised, unflawed stillness that was beyond time, because it remained the same, inexhaustible, unchanging, unexhausted . . . for their moment they were at the heart of eternity, whilst time roared off, for ever far off, towards the rim.[41]

No house, however, seems able to hold two deities forever, and "gradually they were pushed away from the supreme center . . . towards the noise and friction."[42] Anna awakens from her honeymoon hungry, anxious to walk once more in the outside world, the world of tea parties, the world Will wanted to have done with: "Was she not forfeiting the reality, the one reality, for all that was shallow and worthless?"[43] The more he insists that she preserve his divine illusion, the more he becomes to her a "dark, almost evil thing, pursuing her, hanging on to her, burdening her."[44] She grows to fear him:

He seemed to lacerate her sensitive femaleness. He seemed to hurt her womb, to take pleasure in torturing her. . . . Nothing could touch him—he could only absorb things into his own self."[45]

Will's earlier lighthearted wonderment at the change worked in him by marriage, "Indeed, it was true as they said, that a man wasn't born before he was married,"[46] was an ironic prelude for what was to come. Through most of the second part of the novel, Lawrence is interested in describing the birth of Will Brangwen, a birth that will involve the death of a god.

In the early, posthoneymoon days of the marriage, Will's behavior toward Anna is almost without relief that of a leach or fetus, always draining from her her life's blood. Her way of striking back is to whittle away at the religious attachments that prevent Will from worshipping at her shrine. Finally she attacks his woodcut: "It is impudence to say that Woman was made out

of Man's body . . . when every man is born of woman!"[47] Deft-
ly she has fingered his inclination to play the part of the deity;
she has revealed him to himself at the precise moment she refuses
to be his creation, when she is most *other* from him. Enraged one
day he chopped up his masterpiece and put it on the fire, fore-
shadowing thereby the resolution of their problem. The destruction of his masterpiece marks his abandonment of any attempt to
be Anna's master.

When Anna discovers what Will has done, she weeps bitter-
ly, and presently realizes that she is with child. In fact, she is
pregnant with Ursula. In figure, she is laden with Will. In revealing Will to himself, she becomes the way for him to become possessed of himself. When he learns to be free of her, he will be
born a *man*. Then will he recognize her as woman. Then their
marriage will be the kind of covenant the rainbow aptly signifies.

When first Anna tells Will that she is with child, he feels
cut off:

> He was ridden by the awful sense of his own limitation.
> It was as if he ended uncompleted, as yet uncreated on the
> darkness, and he wanted her to come and liberate him into
> the whole.
> But she was complete in herself, and he was ashamed
> of his need . . .[48]

Being ashamed, he was more cruel. Unable to share her exulta-
tion with him, one day she lifted "her hands and her body to the
Unseen, to the unseen Creator who had chosen her, to Whom she
belonged,"[49] took off her clothes, and danced. One day Will sees
her so:

> And she lifted her hands and danced again, to annul
> him . . . dancing to his non-existence, dancing herself to the
> Lord, to exultation.
> . . . He felt he was being burned alive. . . . The vision of
> her tormented him all the days of his life, as she had been
> then, a strange, exalted thing having no relation to him.[50]

He comes to realize that "for his soul's sake, for his manhood's sake, he must be able to leave her."[51] Yet life without Anna seemed to him "a horrible welter, everything jostling in a meaningless, dark, fathomless flood. . . . Yet she was pushing him off from her."[52] Will's birth is almost at hand now.

> And at length, after a grey and livid and ghastly period, he relaxed, something gave way in him. He let go, he did not care what became of him . . . he would force her no more. . . . He recognized at length his own limitation and the limitation of his power. . . . She had given him a new, deeper freedom. The world might be a welter of uncertainty, but he was himself now. He had come into his own existence. He was born for a second time, born at last unto himself, out of the vast body of humanity. . . . Before he had only existed in so far as he had relations with another being. Now he had an absolute self—as well as a relative self.[53]

So Will issues forth from Anna's womb like a man rather than from the womb of his mystic cathedral like a God. Will's journey to manhood meant the death of divine pretensions and illusions.

Anna, too, had her illusions, and she too has a journey to make:

> She was straining her eyes to something beyond. And from her Pisgah mount, which she had attained, what could she see? A faint, gleaming horizon, a long way off, and a rainbow like an archway, a shadow-door with faintly coloured coping above it . . .
> There was something beyond her. But why must she start on the journey? She stood so safely in the Pisgah mountain.
> With satisfaction she relinquished the adventure to the unknown. She was bearing her children.[54]

The journey Anna is summoned to, a journey from an illusion of divinity to the fullness of humanity, is a journey she never makes but which the reader sees in all its detail in the life of Ursula.

On the threshold of womanhood, Ursula wonders why one

must grow up, inherit the responsibility of living an undiscovered life. How was she, in the nothingness, the pathlessness, to take a direction? At her uncle's wedding she too feels the tug of the unknown:

> And how could she start—and how could she let go?
> She must leap from the known into the unknown. . . . Her
> breast strained, as if in bonds.
>
> The music began, and the bonds began to slip. . . .
> One couple after another was washed and absorbed into the
> deep underwater of the dance. . . . It was a vision of the
> depths of the underworld, under the great flood.
>
> There was a wonderful rocking of the darkness, slowly,
> playing lightly on the surface, making the strange, ecstatic
> rippling on the surface of the dance, but underneath only one
> great flood heaving slowly backwards to the verge of oblivion.
>
> As the dance surged heavily on, Ursula was aware of
> some influence looking in upon her. . . . She turned, and
> saw a great white moon looking at her over the hill.[55]

Drawn like the deep to the moon, Ursula longs to receive its power into herself, to become one with its power. Her fascination with, indeed her obsession with, the moon images her search for illumination on her journey into the unknown. Little does she realize that this is an obsession that can annihilate every human relationship, as Lawrence makes evident as he portrays Ursula's relationship to a young army officer on leave, Anton Skrebensky. At first they play at love, hardly realizing the danger they are courting. As time goes on, Skrebensky is drawn to her as a moth is drawn to a candle. He would like to encircle her, to overpower her. Yet

> always she was burning and brilliant and hard as salt, and
> deadly. Yet obstinately, all his flesh burning and corroding,
> as if he were invaded by some consuming, scathing poison,
> still he persisted, thinking at last he might overcome her . . . .
> But . . . gradually his warm, soft iron yielded, and she was

there fierce, corrosive, seething with his destruction . . . destroying him in the kiss. . . . She had triumphed: he was not anymore.[56]

Ursula could not be possessed by Anton or by any man. She was already possessed by the object of her search, which was as real and unreal as the moon. What she failed to see was that the moon received its light and its power from another source; she invested it with a meaning it did not deserve. The illumination she sought was as real and unreal as the moon; and so long as her unbending intent was to become one with it, she could only be destructive to one who sought to bring her life into the circle of his own darkness. Skrebensky's manhood is utterly destroyed in this relationship. His future is the future of the stillborn. Whereas Anna was figuratively pregnant with Will and brought him to his second birth, Ursula "miscarries." Whereas Will had to learn to accept his own limitations to free Anna from an unspoken requirement to complete him, Ursula had to learn to accept her own barrenness:

> Who was she to have a man according to her own desire? It was not for her to create, but to recognize a man created by God. The man should come from the Infinite and she should hail him.[57]

As there is a truth to be discovered in her own barrenness, there is another to be discovered in the ruins of modern life. The image we are left with at the end of *The Rainbow* is one of a contrite spirit, willing at last to accept the frailties of human being, the wasteland of twentieth-century life, the dark cloud. As Ursula gazes out her window at the colliers, "the stiffened bodies of the colliers, which seemed already enclosed in a coffin, . . . their unchanging eyes, the eyes of those who are buried alive . . . the hard, cutting edges of the new houses . . . the old church-tower standing up in hideous obsoleteness above raw new houses . . . the blowing clouds,"[58] she sees a rainbow forming itself:

And the rainbow stood on the earth. She knew that the sordid people who crept hard-scaled and separate on the face of the world's corruption were living still, that the rainbow was arched in their blood and would quiver to life in their spirit, that they would cast off their horny covering of disintegration, that new, clean, naked bodies would issue to a new germination, to a new growth, rising to the light and the wind and the clean rain of heaven. She saw in the rainbow the earth's new architecture, the old brittle corruption of houses and factories swept away, the world built up in a living fabric of Truth, fitting to the over-arching heaven.[59]

The other side of the threefold alienation from God, world, and self, Lawrence suggests, is a new God, a new land, a new self. The mirror of his fiction is the kind one can walk through into an imaginative space in which what has been lost is restored. One becomes possessed of the God, the world, and the self one has let go of.

By the time Lawrence writes *The Man Who Died*, he is past master of his theme, and quite ready to reach for the roots of the threefold alienation that marks modern life. That novel begins with the principal character, identified only as the man who died, awakening from a long and painful sleep. Wrapped in bandages for burial with only his hands free, he wonders who would want to come back from the dead. Finally he rises, silently leaves the tomb, and finds himself once again in the world, "the same as ever, the natural world, thronging with greenness . . . in the world, the natural world of morning and evening, forever undying, from which he had died."[60] The man who died finds himself "in a world that had never died."[61] He takes refuge in the mud hut of a peasant couple, "limited, meagre in their life, without any splendor of gesture and of courage . . . slow inevitable parts of the natural world."[62] The peasants as he sees them "could never die, save to return to earth."[63] Nor was it for him to prevent the peasant from returning to earth in his own good hour, nor to try to "interfere when the earth claims her own."[64]

What Lawrence is depicting here is the situation of the alienated man, the man of heightened consciousness, the man who has his finished life before him, the man who sees his life from birth to death and everything else in relation to that. The alienated man has no place in the world of men who are not conscious of their own difference from deathless nature. The man who constantly has his finished life before him is not at home among people who act as if they shall never die.

The man who died slowly recovers his strength in the sunlight of the peasants' yard and returns to the garden where he had been prematurely buried. There he encounters a woman weeping.

> "Don't touch me, Madeleine," he said. "Not yet! I am not yet healed and in touch with men."[65]

Rejecting her plea to return to his followers, he says:

> "I wanted to be greater than the limits of my hands and feet, so I brought betrayal on myself. . . . Now I can live without striving to sway others anymore. For my reach ends in my fingertips, and my stride is no longer than the ends of my toes. Yet I would embrace multitudes, I who have never truly embraced even one."[66]

Themes Lawrence broached as early as *The Rainbow* again find their way into his fiction. The man with divine pretensions before he had died served the needs of the masses who compelled him to be divine. The man that Madeleine sees now is the death of her dream. It is as if those who are not conscious of their mortality, who do not have their finished lives before them, inevitably lay a compulsion upon others. Their fear of death leads them to use others as shields in one way or another, shields they can put between themselves and the death they fear to consider. This latter note, that self-alienation related to divine pretense has its roots in a refusal to accept mortality, receives new emphasis in *The Man Who Died*. Part One concludes with the man who died, alone now, perceiving the difficulty of the task before him—namely, of coming into touch:

> There was nothing he could touch, for all, in a mad as-
> sertion of the ego, wanted to put a compulsion on him, and
> violate his intrinsic solitude. It was the mania of cities and
> societies and hosts, to lay a compulsion upon a man, upon all
> men. For men and women alike were mad with the egoistic
> fear of their own nothingness. And he thought of his own
> mission, how he had tried to lay a compulsion of love on all
> men . . . there was no contact without a subtle attempt to
> inflict a compulsion.[67]

Here again Lawrence alludes to the peculiar temptation to which men are prone, to deny the distance between men that preserves the possibility of relationships, to compel others to be a means to completion, as if wholeness alone could vanquish death. All men, he suggests, contain within them a mysterious unknown, which might be defined negatively as the possible lives that have been excluded by choices to live one particular life. Man's infinity of possibilities is his share of divinity; to attempt to grasp it, either by refusing to make the choices that a human life entails or by compelling others to relieve one from the awful feeling of incompleteness, fragmentariness, is the temptation that must be overcome if one is to be man. To refuse to make the choices that define a life is to hold fast to the infinite possibilities within, to be godlike. To compel another to complete one is to invest another with a burden no one can bear, to compel the other to be the god with whom one longs for union. The unknown within, the dim reflection of divinity, when it becomes the object of passionate striving, becomes, Lawrence suggests, a lure and an illusion; like the moon, its light comes from another source and one who seeks its power is as one bewitched.

The man who died has known what it is like to be invested with more than human expectations. He longs to discover someone who will love him as a man.

The story resumes on the coast of the Mediterranean at the Temple of Isis, not Isis Mother of Horus, but Isis in Search, Isis who

> was looking for the fragments of the dead Osiris, dead and scattered asunder, dead, torn apart, and thrown in fragments over the wide world. And she must find his hands and his feet, his heart, his thighs, his head, his belly, she must gather him together and fold her arms round the re-assembled body till it became warm again, and roused to life, and could embrace her, and could fecundate her womb.[68]

There the man who died encounters the woman of the Temple who for seven years had served this mystery. Once she had asked a philosopher, "Are all women born to be given to men?" The old man had answered:

> "Rare women wait for the re-born man. For the lotus, as you know, will not answer to all the bright heat of the sun. But she curves her dark, hidden head in the depths, and stirs not. Till in the night, one of these rare, invisible suns that have been killed and shine no more . . . send its rare, purple rays out into the night. To these the lotus stirs . . . and opens with an expansion no other flower possesses. . . . But for the golden brief day-suns of show such as Antony, and for the hard winter suns of power, such as Caesar, the lotus stirs not. . . . Ah, I tell you, wait for the reborn and wait for the bud to stir."[69]

When she beholds the scars of the man who died, the testimony of his suffering, she becomes convinced he is Osiris, the dead whom Isis might restore to life, and she invites him to stay awhile with Isis. He recoils:

> Dare I come into touch? For this is further than death. I have dared to let them lay hands on me and put me to death. But dare I come into this tender touch of life? Oh, this is harder—[70]

He spends the day troubled, wondering whether he will give himself into touch and watching people move like busy ants through the routines of their day.

> It was the life of the little day, the life of the little people. And the man who had died said to himself: "Unless we encompass it in the greater day, and set the little life in the circle of the greater life, all is disaster."[71]

The woman of the Temple comes again and he agrees to meet her, enmeshed in new sensations. "Suns beyond suns had dipped her in mysterious fire, the mysterious fire of a potent woman, and to touch her was like touching the sun."[72] He felt desperate, faced by the demand of life and burdened still by his death. In the dark and fragrant Temple, she beholds the ghost of death in him, "the shadow of the grey grisly wing of death triumphant."[73] She anoints his wounds and the wail within him grows dim.

Yet at first she seems to him not very different from Madeleine. He says, "Once a woman washed my feet with tears, and wiped them with her hair, and poured on precious ointment."[74] She asks whether his feet were hurt then, and he replies, "No! It was while they were whole."[75] He does not foresee the revelation that is in store for him. Their conversation continues:

> "And did you love her?"
> "Love had passed in her. She only wanted to serve," he replied. "She had been a prostitute."
> "And did you let her serve you?" she asked.
> "Yes."
> *"Did you let her serve you with the corpse of her love?"*
> "Ay!"[76]

Suddenly it dawned on him:

> "I asked them all to serve me with the corpse of their love.
> And in the end I offered them only the corpse of my love.
> This is my body—take and eat—my corpse—"[77]

When the priestess shatters thus his illusion that she is but another Madeleine, when he suddenly finds himself in the presence of an *other* who is not fostering his self-delusion, he is revealed to himself, brought finally into touch with himself, able now to come into touch with an other. His doubt recedes as she continues to anoint him:

> "I am going to be warm again, and I am going to be whole! . . . She comes to me from the opposite end of the night."[78]

They embrace.

> Then slowly, slowly in the perfect darkness of his inner-man, he felt the stir of something coming. A dawn, a new sun. A new sun was coming up in him, in the perfect inner darkness of himself. He waited for it breathless, quivering with a fearful hope. . . . "Now I am not myself. I am something new."[79]

He returns to the early morning darkness and beholds the starlit sea:

> Now the world is one flower of many petalled dark-nesses, and I am its perfume as in a touch. . . . This is the great atonement, the being in touch. The grey sea and the rain, the wet narcissus and the woman I wait for, the invisible Isis and the unseen sun are all in touch and at one.[80]

Lawrence does not conclude here. There come those who would turn the man who died over to the Roman authorities. Eluding them, he leaves her. But now he is in touch, and she bears within her his new life.

Both in *The Rainbow* and in *The Man Who Died* Lawrence insists that something like death must be undergone by anyone who truly lives. In every instance the crisis situation is established when a person confronts an *other*, someone who cannot or will not be an extension of that person. The very presence of an *other* marks a boundary for the self and puts the self in relation to the unknown, the strange, the alien. But the self does not wish to be bounded; its reach is infinite, it would be divine. The presence of an other, then, is alienating, both because the self confronts the unknown and because the self is thrown back upon itself in its limits—limits no self wishes to acknowledge. In *The Man Who Died* Lawrence identifies the source of alienation's repulsion in the universal fear of death, the supreme limit that defines the human condition and led the Greeks to call men "mortals."

Yet Lawrence's point is that the confrontation with an other which throws one back upon one's limitations need not be the death of one. Rather it is the death of one's illusions. When freed from those illusions, the self is for the first time self-possessed and for the first time ripe for a lasting human relationship. The presence of an other acknowledged as an other is the condition for the discovery of the self freed from illusion. So what is on the one hand something like a death—the death of illusion—is on the other hand something like a second birth—the birth of a new self. When once a person realizes he need not master the other, dissolve the unknown, he learns that he can live with the other, the unknown in his midst. When he lets the other be other, when he releases the other from the pressure of his need to absorb the other, he is not devoured by the other, as he fears, but suddenly finds the other opening out as a new self, or world, or God to explore.

Before moving to a consideration of the fiction of John Barth, we should note finally that Lawrence's stories not only provided him with an opportunity to see deeply into the twentieth-century experience of alienation from God, world, and self, but also afforded him an opportunity to appropriate the honored stories of his religious tradition, stories that he could no longer be simply *in*. The very distance Lawrence felt between himself and the gospels allowed him to discover in them a truth he personally could embrace. It is doubtful that one whose imagination is not alienated, one who is not familiar with the artificial character of stories, would ever be able to experience that distance or the possibilities created by that very distance. In a curious way, Lawrence suggests that centuries of Christians have become too familiar with the gospels, compelling the gospels to satisfy their mean human needs rather than allowing their strangeness to challenge their self-understanding and thereby really change them. Hence I take it that *The Man Who Died*, rightly considered, is Lawrence's deliberate attempt to shock the Christian reader out of his complacent inclination to domesticate the gospels so that once again they might become strange and, thereby, occasions for personal transformation and personal appropriation. In such a way the storyteller who quite consciously contrives fictions and who is acquainted with the infinite variety of stories he might tell hits upon the one type of story that offers a way through the maze. It is neither the story of the simple soul who is so involved in his tale that he cannot see around it nor the story of the gnostic who mistakes it for revealed truth. It is a contrived fiction, but for all that, it has a very serious point. It is not just another story, another mirror in a labyrinth of mirrors. The mirror of Lawrence's fiction, meant to reflect the alienation of twentieth-century life, is meant to be the kind of mirror one walks *through*. Lawrence creates an imaginative space through which to explore man's alienation from his God, his world, his self, and his religious stories in order to return to the toil of twentieth-century living possessed of a new self and a new vision.

C.   JOHN BARTH

More recent writers are not so sanguine about the power of imagination to blaze a way through the maze. One of the clearest contemporary reflections of the plight of imagination's increased alienation is John Barth's volume of short stories titled *Lost in the Funhouse*. The first story, "Night-Sea Journey," begins:

> "One way or another, no matter which theory of our
> journey is correct, it's myself I address; to whom I rehearse

as to a stranger our history and condition, and will disclose
my secret hope though I sink for it.

　　"Is the journey my invention? Do the night, the sea,
exist at all, I ask myself, apart from my experience of them?
. . .

　　"My trouble is, I lack conviction. Many accounts of our
situation seem plausible to me—where and what we are,
why we swim and whither . . ."[81]

The modern predicament could hardly be more clearly imaged. A
world that is of necessity a mediated world is a world we compose
even as a writer composes a fiction; it is inevitably a fabrication,
and everything and everyone in it can be seen as part of a fiction.

　　What is most notable about the stories that fill Barth's
"funhouse" is not the variety of accounts of the human situation
or metaphors for the journey, but the variety of ways Barth
images the same predicament. "My trouble is, I lack conviction."[82] Earlier we had occasion to note Maritain's notion of
myth as a story that embodies faith or conviction. Where there is
no faith or conviction, there is no myth. There is, however, fiction. The point is not that either myth or fiction is false, but that
the imagination telling the stories is differently situated. Innocent
imagination is *in* the story. Alienated imagination is dislocated.
Even the self it addresses is a stranger. What is remarkable about
the group of stories in *Lost in the Funhouse* is the virtuosity with
which the plight of alienated imagination is displayed. Each story
is like another mirror, or another room, of the same funhouse.
Within the volume, though the dominant metaphor of funhouse
places certain constraints upon the imagination, there are mirrors
or rooms of various sorts that more or less faithfully reflect the
moods of someone lost in the maze.

　　One of the grimmest, "Auto-biography: A Self-Recorded
Fiction," turns out to be the autobiography of a tape-recording
whose last words are its last words. The extended metaphor of the
mechanical voice sets up the dark humor of:

I wonder if I repeat myself. One-track minds may lead
to their origins. Perhaps I'm still in utero, hung up in deliv-
ery; my exposition and the rest merely foreshadow what's to
come, the argument for an interrupted pregnancy.

Womb, coffin, can—in any case, from my viewless
viewpoint I see no point in going further.[83]

Here there is offered no hope of emerging from a labyrinth of
mirrors; the cave is womb and tomb and one is headed not
toward the light and rebirth but, like worm or recording, for the
can. His last words are his last words, and the reader's laughter
rattles in his throat.

Another story, another mood. In "Water-Message," a very
sensitive and self-conscious lad named Ambrose recovers a message in a bottle that reads "To whom it may concern" signed
"Yours truly" but containing no message and no signature. His
seven-year-old friend Perse had asked, "Where in the *world* do
you think it came from?" "Anywhere," Ambrose had replied.
There is apparently no world-message to remove Ambrose from
his world-inventing, a preoccupation of his with which the reader
has become familiar in the course of the story as time and again
Ambrose moves in and out of his fantasies. But the story ends on
a different note from that of "Auto-biography." Its last words are
not "last words" but

. . . some corner of his mind remarked that those shiny bits
in the paper's texture were splinters of wood pulp. Often as
he'd seen them in the leaves of cheap tablets, he had not
hitherto embraced that fact.[84]

In a world mediated by language, in a world that can be cut in an
infinite number of ways, focussed through an inexhaustible supply
of lenses, it might seem that ultimately words come to nothing,
that every attempt to say something significant is frustrated by the
sheer multiplicity of mediations. Because we can say everything,
we in fact say nothing. Then every story, every fiction, comes to
be a note in a bottle that reads "To whom it may concern" signed

"Yours truly" but containing no message and no signature. The feeling that someone has to fill in the blank, say something significant, noble as it is, has no place in the space of this story. It would be an intolerable burden for any writer to think that his own poor composition must surpass all that has already been written, all that has come to nothing. But what Barth suggests in the last words of this story is that there is something in the texture of the paper itself—metaphorically, in stories themselves, even stories whose words come to nothing—that is sturdy enough, endurable enough. Stories don't have to *say* something profound to be significant. Their very *being* signifies far more than their words can hope to convey. This is the kind of thought that frees the writer to "fill in the blank" even though his words come to nothing. Perhaps the funhouse isn't so bad!

The title story, "Lost in the Funhouse," begins:

> For whom is the funhouse fun? Perhaps for lovers. For Ambrose it is *a place of fear and confusion.*[85]

In this story, the narrative is frequently interrupted by comments coming from some unknown source, comments like "Italics are also employed, in fiction stories especially, for 'outside,' intrusive, or artificial voices, such as radio announcements, the texts of telegrams and newspaper articles, et cetera. They should be used *sparingly.*" (Sic)[86] Gimmicks of this sort are not only humorous; they serve to create the effect of artificial voices and sounds that fill the various chambers of the funhouse. They also permit the "all-knowing author" to become insinuated in the story through his musings and to be linked by way of psychological association to the protagonist, Ambrose. The self-consciousness that marks Ambrose also marks the all-seeing author. *And both all-seeing author and Ambrose are to be distinguished from John Barth.*

Within the narrative, thirteen-year-old Ambrose is presented as *en route* to Ocean City's amusement park with his parents, older brother Peter, Uncle Karl and "Magda G———, age

fourteen, a pretty girl and exquisite young lady, who lived not far
from them on B_____ Street . . ."[87] The constant intrusions of
the fusty author, who seems to be having a difficult time getting
anywhere with his story, produce the funhouse effect long before
Ambrose and his coterie arrive at Ocean City. At one point the
all-knowing author laments "We haven't even reached Ocean
City yet: we will never get out of the funhouse."[88] If the all-
knowing author becomes effectively insinuated into the mirror-
maze through this strategy, the reader does, too. The maze of the
story reflects in pale tones the maze of life and gives rise to the
haunting suspicion that fiction *is* the figure and form of life. The
problems besetting the fiction writer cover the same range as
those besetting anyone who has a story to get on with. Since the
fiction writer can author (father?) any story, possible stories, like
possible lives, seem both endless and pointless. But, then, what
about a story about someone lost in a maze? Would that be any
different? Barth apparently thinks it would be—in fact, that is
what *Lost in the Funhouse* is all about.

Almost from the time they arrive at Ocean City, Ambrose
"loses" himself in a fantasy funhouse, one that fascinates him
roughly as Magda G_____ fascinates him, yet which also terrifies him—roughly as Magda G_____ terrifies him? He seems
fascinated by the imaginative prospect of *finding himself lost*. The
funhouse becomes for him a microcosm first of the amusement
park, then of Ocean City:

> The faded distorting mirrors beside Fat May ["the
> Laughing Lady who advertized the funhouse. Larger than
> life, Fat May mechanically shook, rocked on her heels,
> slapped her thighs while recorded laughter—uproarious, fe-
> male—came amplified from a hidden loudspeaker."];[89] the
> impossibility of choosing a mount when one had but a single
> ride on the great carrousel; the *vertigo attendant on his*
> *recognition* that Ocean City was worn out, the place of fa-
> thers and grandfathers, straw-boatered men and parasoled la-
> dies survived by their amusements . . . the girls were upend-

ed and their boyfriends and others could see up their dresses
if they cared to. Which was the whole point, Ambrose realized. Of the entire funhouse! If you looked around, you
noticed that almost all the people on the boardwalk were
paired off into couples except the small children; in a way,
that was the whole point of Ocean City! If you had X-ray
eyes and could see everything going on at that instant under
the boardwalk and in all the hotel rooms and cars and
alleyways, you'd realize that all that normally *showed*, like
restaurants and dance halls and clothing and test-your-
strength machines, was merely preparation and intermission.
Fat May screamed.[90]

Some stream of consciousness for a thirteen-year-old! But, then,
as if anticipating the reader's reaction, Barth's all-knowing author
had just finished reminding him that, regarding Ambrose,

> people don't know what to make of him, he doesn't know
> what to make of himself, he's only thirteen, *athletically and
> socially inept* . . . he understands more than he should, the
> world winks at him through its objects, grabs grinning at his
> coat.[91]

In the passage that follows Fat May's scream, it isn't clear
whether Ambrose has entered the funhouse in fantasy or in fact.
Ambrose's query, "Anybody know where the heck we are?"[92]
could as easily be the reader's—or the author's, who is trying to
get out of his story. Who is it who

> . . . stood rigid for hours it seemed like, scarcely respiring.
> His future was shockingly clear, in outline. [Barth *delights* in
> double and triple entendres.] He tried holding his breath to
> the point of unconsciousness. There ought to be a button you
> could push to end your life absolutely without pain; disap-
> pear in a flick, like turning out a light. He would push it in-
> stantly![93]

How get through the maze, how finish the story, how live—all
three questions merge in the continuing narrative.

"With incredible nerve and to everyone's surprise,"[94]

Ambrose invites Magda to go with him through the funhouse. In fact or in fantasy? the reader wonders. In any case, Ambrose lapses again into his musings: "His father should have taken him aside and said: 'There is a simple secret to getting through the funhouse . . .' "[95] As he muses further, his father never has the chance to reveal the secret. His father's last "words," *on the contrary*, italicized to alert the reader to the presence of the intruding all-knowing author, precede:

> If you knew all the stories behind all the people on the boardwalk, you'd see that *nothing* was what it looked like. Husbands and wives often hated each other; parents didn't necessarily love their children; et cetera. A child took things for granted because he had nothing to compare his life to and everybody acted as if things were as they should be. Therefore each saw himself as the hero of the story, when the truth might turn out to be that he's the villain, or the coward. And there wasn't one thing you could do about it![96]

Earlier, the all-knowing author had stated "The more closely an author identifies with the narrator, literally or metaphorically, the less advisable it is, as a rule, to use the first-person narrative viewpoint."[97] The effect here of the merging of Ambrose and narrator once again sets up the linked problems of Ambrose's getting through the maze, of the author's getting out of his story, and of the person's living in the face of contending metaphors that would inform his fiction.

At last they go in. Ambrose immediately drops his name-coin among tumbling couples. Then an interesting thing happens. The all-knowing author, whose intrusions up until now have been calculated to fuse his own "personality" with Ambrose's, intrudes again, but this time to *dissociate* himself from Ambrose. He remarks:

> In the maze two important things happened. First, our hero found a name-coin someone else had lost or discarded: AMBROSE . . .[98]

For the first time a wedge is driven between "our hero" and Ambrose. The author is trying to extricate himself from his fic-tion. Barth, too, wishes to announce his independence from the fate both of Ambrose *and* of the author. The second thing that happened, however, brings the all-knowing author back into rela-tion to Ambrose:

> Second, as he wondered at the endless replication of his image in the mirrors, second as he *lost himself in the reflec-tion* that the necessity for an observor makes perfect observa-tion impossible . . . he heard Peter and Magda chuckling somewhere together in the maze.[99]

The all-knowing author is not Ambrose, yet cannot seem to get along without Ambrose. Will he ever get out? Will the author get himself out of the story? Ambrose stands quietly as his brother and Magda hurrah their discovery of the exit. "Then he set his mouth and followed after, as he supposed, took a wrong turn, strayed into the pass *wherein he lingers yet.*"[100] Again the all-knowing author intrusively belabors the problem he is having with his fiction. It almost seems as if now he, as distinct from Ambrose, is musing about endings when he says:

> This can't go on much longer; it can go on forever. He died telling stories to himself in the dark; years later, when that vast unsuspected area of the funhouse came to light, the first expedition found his skeleton in one of its labyrinthine corridors and mistook it for part of the entertainment. He died of starvation telling himself stories in the dark . . .[101]

As his musings move from the dramatic to the melodramatic, from the sublime to the ridiculous, he concludes:

> The climax of the story must be its protagonist's discov-ery of a way to get through the funhouse. But he has found none, may have ceased to search.[102]

At this point, Ambrose indeed lingers yet in the funhouse. But the all-knowing author, this story's protagonist, who finds a name-coin in Ambrose, but who also momentarily dissociates himself from Ambrose, has—climactically—stumbled on the way out. Ambrose comes limping after. Ambrose

> envisions a truly astonishing funhouse, incredibly complex yet utterly controlled from a great central switchboard like the console of a pipe-organ. Nobody had enough imagination. He could design such a place himself, wiring and all, and he's only thirteen years old. He would be its operator: panel lights would show what was in every cranny of its cunning of its multifarious vastness; a switch-flick would ease this fellow's way, complicate that's, to balance things out; if anyone seemed lost or frightened, all the operator had to do was.
>
> He wishes he had never entered the funhouse. But he has. Then he wishes he were dead. But he's not. Therefore he will construct funhouses for others and be their secret operator—though he would rather be among the lovers for whom funhouses are designed.[103]

The climactic discovery of a way through the funhouse is linked to the success of the all-knowing author in dissociating himself from his fictional character. In recognizing his fictional presence *and* his independence from his fictional representative, he succeeds in getting himself out of his story, of going on living after finishing his story.

The fictional breakthrough of "Lost in the Funhouse" is masterfully repeated in "Life-Story." After advising the reader of his decision to tell his tale in a "conservative, 'realistic,' unselfconscious way," the author confesses:

> He being by vocation an author of novels and stories it was perhaps inevitable that one afternoon the possibility would occur to the writer of these lines that his own life might be a fiction, in which he was the leading or an accessory character.[104]

So it is that the vehicle for his story vouchsafed itself: "D comes

to suspect that the world is a novel, himself a fictional per-
sonage."[105] Moreover,

> since D is writing a fictional account of this conviction he
> has indisputably a fictional existence in his account, replicat-
> ing what he suspects to be his own situation. Moreover E,
> hero of D's account, is said to be writing a similar account,
> and so the replication is in both ontological directions, et ce-
> tera.[106]

Having recognized his vehicle, the author of "Life Story"
muses on its questionability, so "self-conscious," "fashionably
solipsistic," "unoriginal—in fact a convention of twentieth-century literature."[107] Some "realistic" touch when he adds:

> Another story about a writer writing a story! . . .
> Who doesn't prefer art that . . . doesn't continually pro-
> claim "Don't forget I'm an artifice!"[108]

The author of "Life Story" rather preferred straightforward tales
of adventure. C flings away his manuscript and pushes through
his study doors to go out on the terrace. The author of "Life
Story" finds the prospect of being a fictional character in his least
favorite kind of fiction disquieting. B calls on a literary acquaintance who offers:

> To write merely C comes to suspect that the world is a
> novel, himself a fictional personage is but to introduce the
> vehicle; the next step must be to initiate its uphill motion by
> establishing and complicating some conflict. I would advise
> in addition the eschewal of overt and self-conscious discus-
> sion of the narrative process.[109]

With this advice and with the identification of the literary
acquaintance as B_____, a convention of the nineteenth-century
novels, the reader finally has a clue to the sequential relation of
writers. B_____, lover of paradox, conventionally affects a realistic posture by authorial intrusion. In the present context, the intrusion would be, presumably, to eschew overt and self-conscious

discussion of the narrative process. C, the twentieth-century writer, appears doomed to write stories about a writer writing a story.
The process seems to be the endlessly repeating cycle of apparent
realism (in fact artifice) followed by apparent artifice (in fact realism). Hence, as "Life Story" progresses (and as we begin to see
that the "life" being storied here covers quite a spectrum of
lives), G predictably declares his preference to be in a "rousing
good yarn as they say, not some piece of avant-garde pre-
ciousness."[110] J, on the contrary, provokes him to reflect, "If he
can only get K through his story . . .; if he can only retain his
self-possession to the end of this sentence; not go mad; not destroy himself and/or others."[111] The pattern of seemingly endless
repetitions puts the present writer in a bind, since, after all, all the
achievements of his predecessors and of his successors are painful-
ly present in a consciousness that could hardly be better signified
than by the "third-person omniscient" authorial voice. "Why
could he not begin his story afresh X wondered . . ."[112]

The author begins again, admitting his suspicion that the
medium and genre in which he worked, not to mention the society in which he persisted and the body he inhabited, were mori-
bund if not already dead. Indeed, if he is but a character in a fiction, he *is* in a sense finished. If he relates to others as if they are
lesser characters in a fiction of which he is the hero, they too are
finished. The only way to break out of the endless cycle of stories
—the only way to get his author out of this story—is to distinguish sharply between the fictional figure and the living person
who refuses to be finished in a fiction. The doubt-besieged author
finally slips out of his story on a paradoxical note. His wife comes
to him in his study at midnight to wish him, significantly, "Happy
Birthday, . . . kissing him et cetera to obstruct his view of the
end of the sentence he was nearing the end of, playfully refusing
to be nay-said so that in fact he did at last as did his fictional
character end his ending story endless by interruption, cap his pen
. . ."[113] Just before, he had protested his ability to demonstrate

that the story of his life was a work of fact, not fiction:

> Though assaults upon the boundary between life and
> art, reality and dream, were undeniably a staple of his own
> and his century's literature as they'd been of Shakespeare's
> and Cervantes's, yet it was a fact that in the corpus of fiction
> as far as he knew no fictional character had become con-
> vinced as he had that he was a character in a work of fiction.
> This being the case and he having in fact become thus con-
> vinced it followed that his conviction was false.[114]

The paradox is that consciousness of the fictional shape of the life
story frees the person from being frozen in a fiction. When that
consciousness is lacking, it is all the more likely that one would
live *as if* he were the hero of his story. The self-conscious one
perceives he might just as easily be the villain, or the coward. His
very awareness of the variety of postures open to him—signified
in this story by the variety of authorial voices—allows him to slip
out of his stories. The reader who follows Barth through his fictions paradoxically doffs the deceitful garb he may have put on in
his life but which is now exposed in the fictions, and experiences
the movement through the funhouse as Ambrose does, as a kind
of initiation rite of purification. In such fashion Barth takes one
to the very limits of an alienated imagination's possibilities, to the
brink of the domain of "purged imagination."

The only thing that prevents Barth from going beyond the
range of alienated imagination is the constraint exercised by the
dominant "funhouse" metaphor. As one moved from room to
room, from mirror to mirror, one would explore "every cranny of
its cunning of its multifarious vastness"[115] in the light provided
by its operator. No corner of the cave illumined by the firelight of
imagination would go unnoticed. Presumably no human conceit
or deceit would go unexposed. But there seems for alienated
imagination in Barth's instance no interest in moving out of the
cave. Rather would Barth transform it from a place of fear and
confusion into a place for lovers. His intention is not to be free

from earth but to penetrate her, to fecundate her womb.

D. CONCLUSION

Alienated imagination, we have proposed, is an imagination conscious of its own activity. In terms of Plato's cave analogy, it realizes the significance of its turn away from the shadows. It knows that in the firelight of intelligence it encounters things which it has put together and which are, therefore, "mere artifice." It knows that its stories are fictions that it has contrived, fictions which, like mirrors, serve to bring to view every nook and cranny of the cave—as well as the head that is continually getting in the way.

This rather recent development in storytelling was not the product of a theory of literature. Men's doing preceded men's thinking. A new science spawned by a novel technique which itself bore witness to a new freedom vis-à-vis the world led to the theoretical labor of Kant and others. Their philosophic work simply acknowledged an event that had transpired in the life of spirit. Still, the notion that the world is *inescapably* mediated by language could not but have a telling effect on the stories told to the dark. The emergence of the novel in the modern period is consistent with man's new feeling of responsibility for the world he composes.

There is not surprisingly a certain bind the storyteller grown self-conscious feels which earlier storytellers did not know. If all the worlds we can be in are worlds we compose, if we are inescapably in fictions, if in the firelight all we see is mirrored space and our own reflections, for what then may we hope? Are we lost in the funhouse? Shall we ever emerge from out of a labyrinth of mirrors? Are there any stories that haven't already been told that are worth the telling? Would any story make a difference? These are the peculiar questions the modern raises with increasing regularity.

John Barth's way of stepping into the dilemma is to frame it with the funhouse image. His movement through the funhouse of his stories, then, depends upon being able to identify himself in successive fictional aspects in order to shed them, the way one might shed clothes. His fictions become ways of identifying the illusions that prevent one from enjoying the funhouse like a proper lover. Each illusion unmasked is another falsehood stripped away, and the process of stripping is then not unlike a purification rite preparatory for a love feast. The funhouse is not transcended but transformed from a place of confusion and fear into a place for lovers. The point is not to leave the cave, the earth, behind, but to enter into it, to embrace it, to fertilize it. The kind of mirror Barth offers in his fiction is not a magic mirror so much as a mirror that manages to reflect within it every other mirror.

D. H. Lawrence is interested in casting off illusion, too, but in doing so he places much more emphasis on the importance of the presence of an *other* who opens, like a doorway, onto the unknown. His fiction, interestingly, produces precisely this effect upon the reader. His outrageous, deliberately offensive use of the gospels brutally unmasks the conceits of Christians and compels them to return to the gospels with a new sense of their strangeness. He may not convert many readers to his own green vision, but he will assuredly shake them out of their own religious or irreligious complacencies. The essential otherness of the familiar is the way "alienation" is mirrored in Lawrence's fiction; inevitably, then, his fiction points beyond itself. The other becomes a doorway that opens onto the unknown; when one steps into the unknown, one steps through the mirror into an *other* world.

The different emphasis in Barth and in Lawrence is manifest in the different way each relates to stories. Barth's *Giles Goat-Boy* is a tour de force of artifice, a baroque mosaic of all the great stories the imagination has engendered. His hero is carefully endowed with all the qualities one needs to excel on the ideal scale of heroes compiled by the objective researcher. The motifs and symbols of all the great stories are woven together in one grand symphony of sound and fury that comes to nothing. The story delights the person who takes delight in stories for their own sake. The story disappoints the person whose comprehension of the vocation of the storyteller is more expansive than Barth's. D. H. Lawrence would have despised such a story as *Giles Goat-Boy*, though he would have felt no more comfortable than Barth with the honored stories of traditional religion. Lawrence characteristically takes up the stories of an alien tradition and recomposes them in the smithy of his soul. He walks through the mirror of his fiction beyond the labyrinth of mirrors.

Whether one settles down in a funhouse, telling stories to the dark (till death do us part), or becomes a traveller into the unknown, in either case one is exposed, stripped, and stretched. In this respect, alienated imagination at its limits approaches the domain of purged imagination, to which we may now turn.

CHAPTER 4

Clouds

Purged Imagination: Stills Stories,
Lets the Void Be Void

Reconcile yourself to wait in this darkness as long as is necessary, but still go on longing after him whom you love. For if you are to feel him or see him in this life, it must always be in this cloud, in this darkness.

. . . The vigorous working of your imagination, which is always so active when you set yourself to this blind contemplation, must as often be suppressed.[1]

The death of the self . . . is merely the slow cessation of the will's sprints and the intellect's chatter; it is waiting like a hollow bell with stilled tongue.[2]

The most luminous examples of "purged imagination" are to be found among the western Christian mystics. The unknown author of *The Cloud of Unknowing*, the John of the Cross who wrote *Dark Night of the Soul*, the desert fathers, and more recently the author of *Pilgrim at Tinker Creek* are as aware of the activity of imagination as the most self-conscious of fiction writers. They are aware of seeing things through the windows of imagination. But their counsel is to scour the windows, not so much to see more clearly as to be more present to the dark. They know the temptation to illumine the darkness that surrounds the life, to fill the void with imagination. But rather than contrive fictions with which to illumine every nook and cranny of the cave, they would have us still the stories and refuse to fill the void with imagination in order to feel the dark that encompasses our lives and is present the moment we become quiet. Their counsel is not to stay forever in banquet hall or funhouse telling stories to pass the time but rather to go out into the dark and in the dark to feel the emptiness, the void—and there to wait.

What do these phrases mean: to still stories, to refuse to fill the void with imagination, to wait in the dark? And why would anyone offer such counsel?

So far we have considered three kinds of stories: stories we are in unthinkingly, stories we are in with a vengeance, and stories we merely entertain. Smohalla's story is an example of the first kind. Such a story is the frame tale that provides the tacit context for all of a person's experiences. The American success story is a more pedestrian example of a story we might be in without thinking about it, as we take our bearings, make our decisions, size up our neighbors, and take our own measure in terms of "success" and "failure." The kind of story we are in unthinkingly is grist for the mill of a writer like John Barth, whose fictions expose the shape of such a story and put in stark relief the roles we are acting out.

We have also considered stories we are in with a vengeance, stories that offer a powerful resolution of the riddles of human existence and promise to erase the faintest trace of mystery. These are the gnostic stories that fill the void with fantastic visions, the ideologies that first free and then freeze their adherents.

Finally, we have considered stories that entertain and which we can entertain as we wander through a virtual maze of stories on a journey that contains no promises about a resting place or destination. These are the stories that we, like Scheherazade, might tell to pass the time, to stay alive another hour, another day.

To still the stories, then, would be first to stop the momentum of the story that carries us unthinkingly through life and to come to rest for awhile in the stillness. Second, to still stories would be to resist the temptation to fill the silence with "the will's sprints and the intellect's chatter,"[3] with the stories we are in with a vengeance or with stories we entertain with greater sophistication.

Were we to manage to still the stories, we would begin to feel the void, our own emptiness in the face of the unknown. We would be for the moment in our own shadow, searching the empty spaces of the night for a sign, realizing in the end the futility of any attempt to manufacture one. The temptation to fill the void with imagination, to escape the feeling of our own vanity by taking refuge in the will's sprints and the intellect's chatter, would be difficult to resist. To refuse to fill the void with imagination would be to sustain the stillness, to wait in the dark. Whatever for? Annie Dillard writes:

> Not only does something come if you wait, but it pours over you like a waterfall, like a tidal wave. You wait in all naturalness without expectation or hope, emptied, translucent, and that which comes rocks and topples you; it will shear, loose, launch, winnow, grind.[4]

It would be difficult to propose a more beautiful or more powerful *image* than this one for impressing on someone the point of becoming still. Yet Dillard's *Pilgrim at Tinker Creek*, like the writings of the mystics, abounds in such images. Dillard just a few lines later writes:

> I stand under wiped skies directly, naked, without intercessors. Frost winds have lofted my body's bones with all their restless sprints to an airborne raven's glide. I am buoyed by a calm and effortless longing, an angled pitch of

the will, like the set of the wings of the monarch [butterfly]
which climbed a hill by falling still.[5]

Similarly, *The Cloud of Unknowing* is filled with counsels like
"just as the cloud of unknowing is as it were above you, between
you and God, so you must also put a cloud of forgetting beneath
you and all creation."[6] Such counsel reduces to "put out of your
inner space everything that would crowd into it: things, images,
words, stories, worldly concerns. Make of yourself a desert." This
is the route followed by those who literally put themselves in the
desert in the third century A.D. Their legacy includes sayings like
"As a fish must return to the sea, so we must to our cell: lest it
befall that by tarrying without, we forget the watch within,"[7] and
"Who sits in solitude and is quiet hath escaped from three wars:
hearing, speaking, and seeing: yet against one thing shall he continually battle: that is, his own heart."[8]

The imagination is richly present in all these spiritual writings, but the intention of the writer differs profoundly from the
intention of other writers we have considered. The purged imagination is more interested in making some space in the life of the
person who listens than it is in filling it. More accurately, the
purged imagination encourages the listener to become present to
the infinite space of the soul's dark night (that is never more than
a breath away) precisely by refusing to fill that space with fancy.
In short, imagination is invoked to free one from imagination's
folly.

When this paradoxical operation of imagination has been
understood, it comes as less of a surprise that the same imagination that counsels the stilling of stories has gifted western literature with one of the greatest stories ever told. That story blazed a
new path in storytelling, virtually creating a new genre. While it
displayed the genius of the artificer, it was not artifice. The shape
of the story was the shape of events that really happened. Imagination exercised an unheard-of restraint as it compelled the contours of the narrative to conform to the contours of a life. Auto-

biography was born with Augustine's *Confessions*, but autobiography in a very special sense. For while Augustine was narrating the events of the life and registering his relation to the events of his life, Augustine the narrator composed his work in the stillness—deliberately. Hence, even though the stuff of his story is comprised of the givens of his life, he is primarily concerned to tell God's story, the story of the God who comes in the dark night to disclose himself in the events of the life. If the western mystics are the most luminous examples of purified imagination, Augustine alone seems to have grasped the import of an asceticism of imagination for storytelling.

To hear God's speech in the events of his life, Augustine needed to become still, to be freed from the distractions that flooded into his life. Becoming quiet, ridding his "house" of the clutter, transforming his inner space into a house of prayer was the essential preparation for this work which he (who surely attended to the meaning of words) called "confessions." The work he composed required an unheard-of asceticism of imagination. Augustine insisted on this kind of restraint in order to display how one might rightly know God and, as a result, oneself in one's depth. He shows the principal obstacles to be overcome by anyone whose journey in the dark is a journey to God.

Looking back on his life from the perspective of one who has heard God's word in his lifetime, Augustine located two obstacles in the path of the pilgrim, two distractions that need to be removed if one is to advance in the spiritual life. The first distraction was, quite simply, noise. Augustine found in the turmoil of his adolescent sexual life the adequate image to display the problem. At this point, Augustine's life was full of noise, a lot of sound and fury signifying nothing. This frame of mind is well imaged by the adolescent, but it is not confined to the adolescent. Augustine the artificer has seized upon a real period of turbulence in order to image a universal condition that must be surmounted if the pilgrim is to move forward. What matters is the recognition that, when there was noise in his life, he had no ear for God's speech. He could not hear it because of all the noise. The events of his life followed willy-nilly, one upon the other, without order, without sense, without distinction. In this frame of mind, even the exceptional events of birth, death, and marriage tend to become lost in the flow, in the flood, in the noise, in the clutter. Imagination's habitual orientation is calculated to absorb experiences indiscriminately so that none stand out. Life goes on, but nothing *happens*. When the imaginative context for every event is the senseless, pointless, endless flow of the everyday, there is a kind of noise in the life that blocks the kind of communication an older Augustine referred to when he wrote:

> How presumptuous it was of me to say that you were silent, my God. . . . all the while you were speaking to me through her, and when I disregarded her, your handmaid, I was disregarding you, though I was both her son and your servant.[9]

Not only can one's habitual orientation screen out God's speech; it is also possible to enter into a kind of perverse pact by conspiring to fill one's life with noise, with nonsense, with distractions that work to increase the resistance to the counsel to become still. Only when one attempts to become still, to stop the clatter and get rid of the clutter, does one realize how powerful that resistance has grown. Occasionally a birth, more frequently a death, sweeps the resistance aside, but with astonishing regularity the habitual orientation returns, preserving the monotonous consistency of the everyday, the marvel-less world in which nothing happens.

Cut off from any lively contact with God, that is, from God's speech, it is not surprising that the god Augustine believed in at this time was an "empty figment":

> The god I worshipped was my own delusion, and if I tried to find in it a place to rest my burden, there was nothing there to uphold it.[10]

The burden Augustine referred to here was the loss of his friend. Augustine's senseless coursing through the universe was suddenly stopped as the death of his friend compelled him to face his own mortality and the fragility of every living thing. He was transported suddenly to the nether borders of his life, where he felt momentarily the darkness in which his life was sunk. And he was dismayed and appalled at his discovery:

> True or not, the story goes that Orestes and Pylades were ready to die together for each other's sake, because each would rather die than live without the other. But I doubt whether I should have been willing, as they were, to give my life for my friend. I was obsessed by a strange feeling, quite the opposite of theirs, for I was sick and tired of living and yet afraid to die. I suppose that the great love which I had for my friend made me hate and fear death all the more, as though it were the most terrible of enemies, because it had snatched him away from me. I thought that, just as it had seized him, it would seize all others too without warning.[11]

For the moment, Augustine was brought to the abyss. He felt the void and he reeled. He could not stay there long. He fled the town which his friend's spirit haunted and went to Carthage. Other friends consoled him. Their fables filled the void.

Of course in the beginning Augustine did not regard their Manichaean stories as fables, but as wisdom. As we have already seen in the second chapter, the Manichaean did not expect life in this world to satisfy the heart's desire. Life on earth was regarded as a life of exile; one's true home was with the Father of Greatness, and the sooner one withdrew from the enticements of earth, the body's liabilities, the better off one was. Within this perspective, death, even the death of loved ones, had a point: it served as a useful reminder of the situation of exile *out of which one was called.* Only later did Augustine identify the stories of the Manichaeans as fables, "dazzling fantasies, illusions with which the eye deceives the mind."[12] They represented for Augustine a more sinister distraction than the noise and the clutter of life because they willfully distorted the givens of human experience and thereby blocked the channels of divine communication. Having no respect for the sinews of stories, they did not hesitate to tear asunder the honored stories of religion and to perpetrate parodies that pretended to resolve all life's riddles. Augustine made no effort to conceal his contempt when he wrote:

> The dishes they set before me were still loaded with dazzling fantasies, illusions with which the eye deceives the mind . . . I gulped down this food, because I thought it was you. I had no relish for it, because the taste it left in my mouth was not the taste of truth—it could not be, for it was not you but empty sham. And it did not nourish me, but starved me all the more. The food we dream of is very like the food we eat when we are awake, but it does not nourish because it is only a dream. Yet the things they gave me to eat were not in the least like you, as now I know since you have spoken to me. They were dream substances, mock realities . . . the visionary foods on which I was then fed but not sustained.
> . . . The images we form in our mind's eye, when we picture things that really do exist, are far better than these inventions; and the things themselves are still more certain than the images we form of them. But you are not these things. Neither are you the soul, which is the life of bodies and, since it gives them life, must be better and more certain than they are themselves. But you are the life of souls, the life of lives.[13]

What a contrast are these lines to those he uttered recalling when first he knew God:

> When first I knew you, you raised me up so that I could see that there was something to be seen, but also that I was not yet able to see it. I gazed on you with eyes too weak to resist the dazzle of your splendour. . . . I realized that I was far from you. It was as though I were in a land where all is different from your own and I heard your voice calling

from on high, saying "I am the food of full-grown men.
Grow and you shall feed on me. But you shall not change
me into your own substance, as you do with the food of your
body. Instead you shall be changed into me."[14]

The givens of the created universe did not stand a chance in the
Manichaean imagination, through whose sorcery things and
events were immediately transformed into hierophanic displays.
The sun was more Primal Man than sun; the Milky Way was not
a galaxy but the highway to salvation. The Manichaean stories
revealed the human spark to be of the same stuff as the Father of
Greatness himself. No wonder Mani's imagination sailed to the
stars! No wonder he did not hesitate to wave his wand and wipe
away the sky. No wonder he did not hesitate to rewrite Genesis.
His was the stuff that gods were made of.

It was this exalted sense of self that Augustine repudiated in
the very first lines of his *Confessions* when he insisted, "Man is
one of your creatures, Lord, and his instinct is to praise you."[15] It
is not for man to create, but to recognize the creation of which he
is a part. The perversity of the Manichaean imagination was that
it did everything that could be done to obscure this cardinal
Christian affirmation. It prevented one from grasping with Augustine that God is not like the soul or the life of bodies but like
the life of souls. Imagination is not a share in God's life, but, like
everything else, is a creature held in existence by its creator. It is
not the business of imagination to conjure up a divinity that meets
its specifications, but to become transformed by the God who
creates it and redeems it. Rather than spend one's time in flights
of fancy, one ought to pay proper attention to the things and
events that are real and that, in denying their own divinity, point
beyond themselves to the God who lets them be. The point is not
that imagination is ill-starred, condemned to weave illusions;
rather, imagination is to be "brought low," subdued, so that
when it makes use of the things of God it may find in them a
surer path to the Lord of all creation. The storyteller is not con-

demned, but encouraged to build his stories well, to offer a substantial poetry.

In Augustine's mind, the greatest contrast to the stories of
the Manichaeans were the Holy Scriptures:

> How wonderful are your Scriptures! How profound!
> We see their surface and it attracts us like children. And yet,
> O God, their depth is stupendous. We shudder to peep into
> them, for they inspire in us both the awe of reverence and
> the thrill of love.[16]

In the next breath Augustine remarked that if he were to write a
book that was to be vested with the highest authority he would
model it on the Scriptures, with language at once simple and
profound. The *Confessions* is that book.

In place of the eery, airy speculations of the gnostics are the
profoundly human eye and ear of a writer who knew his neighborhood. "The poverty of our human intellect generally produces
an abundance of words . . .";[17] he might have added that it also
generally produces an abundance of images. To hear we need to
be quiet. Before we break the silence with our speech or fill the
void with our imagination, we need to be still, to return to the
kind of silence that preceded the word of creation. When we
become still like that, things become present; we become present
to the things and events that are *happening*. We take them to
heart. We get to know our neighborhood and the dialect of our
neighbors. The stories we tell have the earthy texture of real
places and real people. They do not distract us from our serious
purpose but make us yet more attentive. That is exactly the sort
of story Augustine is telling.

If in the early books of the *Confessions* Augustine uncovered
the obstacles to the spiritual journey and suggested the kind of
preparation called for if one is ever to know God rightly, in the
eighth book he showed what happens to one who has become attentive. He framed that book with the 115th Psalm and with a
passage from Matthew's gospel (Mt. 11:25, 28-29). There was

one other time when that gospel passage occupied Augustine's attention: on the occasion of his first Christmas sermon. It seems unlikely to have been accidental that the same passage he treated as pastor on the feast of the Nativity was the very one he used to set off from the rest of his story the account of Christ's birth in his life. It was a beautiful artistic touch, alerting the reader to the skillful crafting that characterizes the whole of Book VIII. Yet for all the care he gave to its composition, Augustine did not for a moment distract the reader from the seriousness of the story he was about to tell, the story of his conversion.

On one level, it is a very striking and a very simple story. Augustine was troubled in his heart, wondered why he could not do what he wanted to do, heard a child singing "Take it and read," opened the Scriptures at random to a passage from Paul that spoke directly to his dilemma and gave him a direction. He took the words as God's addressed to him and he obeyed. It is that simple.

Yet, like the Scriptures, there is more to the story than meets the eye. Augustine would never have been in the garden to hear the child's song had he not been troubled by a story about the conversion of two men told him by his countryman Ponticianus, and he would never have picked up the Scriptures prompted by the child's song if he had not earlier heard the story of Antony. It was Antony who wandered into a church, heard the priest read words from Scripture that spoke to his predicament, took them as a personal charge from God, and changed his life. In other words, Augustine's conversion depended upon a story within a story, on the story of Antony contained in Ponticianus' story. One does not have to be John Barth to appreciate the nesting effect of the stories within the story of Augustine's conversion. But Augustine's life story is different from Barth's "Life Story." To be sure, the artificer is at work in both instances. But whereas Barth is drawn to explore metaphorically *a way out of* a fictional and, perhaps, real cul-de-sac, Augustine is concerned to show *a way onto* the "high road to that land of peace, the way that is defended by the care of the heavenly Commander."[18] Whereas the stories within the story of Barth's "Life Story" are contrived stories to be shed like clothes that disguise, the stories within the story of Augustine's conversion are true stories to take with one on one's journey. The stories in Augustine's *Confessions* are not extended metaphors, but condensed revelations that address first not the mind but the heart. We do not try to figure them out or take them apart like pieces of a Chinese puzzle the way we do with Barth's fictions. If we have managed to stop the noise in our life and become still, if we have succeeded in resisting the urge to fill the silence with speech, the void with imagination, we find reflected in Augustine's story and in the stories within his story the deep lake of the heart, of our heart, that is occasionally stirred by the touch of something real. Augustine's story does not provoke our speculations, it does not edify or entertain us; it rather thrusts us back upon ourselves with the charge to become quiet and be stirred. Were we to accept that charge, and were we to tell the story of our stirring, we would be writing our confessions. It would be a story that is at once our life story and the story of the God who came in the dark night when we were still to stir the lake of our heart.

Even to consider the possibility of "confessing" is to question whether any other story would be worth the telling. Should the imagination bother with any other story than the story that lies concealed in the depths of our hearts? Once imagination has become subdued, shall it ever be raised up again? Will it ever soar to the stars?

When we become still, when we turn inward to walk for awhile in the night, in earth's shadow, it is good to remember what Annie Dillard writes about shadows:

> Once, when Tinker Creek had frozen inches thick at a
> wide part near the bridge, I found a pileated woodpecker in
> the sky by its giant shadow flapping blue on the white ice

below. It flew under the neighborhood children's skates; it soared whole and wholly wild though they sliced its wings. I'd like a chunk of that shadow, a pane of freshwater ice to lug with me everywhere, fluttering huge under my arm, to use as the Eskimos did for a window on the world. Shadow is the blue patch where the light doesn't hit. It is mystery itself . . .[19]

And

> The shadow's the thing. Outside shadows are blue, I read, because they are lighted by the blue sky and not the yellow sun. Their blueness bespeaks infinitesimal particles scattered down inestimable distance. Muslims, whose religion bans representational art as idolatrous, don't observe the rule strictly; but they do forbid sculpture, because it casts a shadow. So shadows define the real. If I no longer see shadows as "dark marks" as do the newly sighted, then I see them as making some sort of sense of the light. They give the light distance; they put it in its place. They inform my eyes of my location here, here O Israel, here in the world's flawed sculpture, here in the flickering shade of the nothingness between me and the light.
>
> Now that the shadow has dissolved the heaven's blue dome, I can see Andromeda again . . .[20]

Neither Dillard nor Dante were cut out to be Muslims. When they stand in earth's shadow, in the night, in the stillness, they look up. They see pileated woodpecker. They see the stars whose splendor comes to view only when one stands in earth's shadow, in the night. They go forth in the dark to ascend to the stars. What they tell brings us to a consideration of imagination restored: "sanctified imagination."

CHAPTER 5

Stars

Sanctified Imagination: Sounds Songs, Rings Out Realities

O you that follow in light cockle-shells,
    For the song's sake, my ship that sails before,
    Carving her course and singing as she sails,
Turn back and seek the safety of the shore;
    Tempt not the deep, lest, losing unawares
    Me and yourselves, you come to port no more.
Ocean as yet undared my vessel dares;
    Apollo steers, Minerva lends the breeze,
    And the nine Muses point me to the Bears.
But you, rare souls, that have reached up to seize
    Betimes the bread of angels, food for men
    To live on here, whereof no surfeit is,
You may commit your bark to the main,
    Hard on my keel, where ridge and furrow flee
    Ere the vext waters level out again.[1]

These bold words opening the second canto of Dante's *Paradiso* herald a new poetic and a new vantage point for imagination. We might well wonder from where this daring speech

112

issues. What seas have already been charted by this voyager who ventures into the uncharted waters of an "ocean as yet un-dared"?[2]

The vantage point Dante occupies when he writes the second canto can be quickly glimpsed by adverting to the cantos that immediately precede it. The logging of the journey that leads to the vantage point of "sanctified imagination" requires a more thorough examination, but it has the advantage of allowing us to bring together some of the themes that have been emerging from the beginning of our inquiry.

Where is Dante when he issues the warning with which we opened this chapter?

> Ocean as yet undared my vessel dares;
> Apollo steers . . .[3]

The reference to Apollo here reminds us that in the first canto of the *Paradiso* it was Apollo and not the Muses whom Dante invoked. The Muses sufficed for the writing of the *Inferno* and the *Purgatorio*, but for the writing of the *Paradiso* Dante calls upon Apollo himself:

> Gracious Apollo! in this crowning test
> Make me conduit that thy power runs through![4]

Dante's appeal is not to the Muses who inspire poets but to Apollo. The power that both sustains things on earth and permits them to be seen is the power Dante invokes to power his poetry. Dante's vantage point is elevated indeed.

We get a further glimpse of his vantage point when, later in the first canto, Dante writes:

> When Beatrice, intent upon the sun,
>> Turned leftward, and so stood and gazed before;
>> No eagle e'er so fixed his eyes thereon.
> And, as the second ray doth evermore
>> Strike from the first and dart back up again,
>> Just as the peregrine will swoop and soar,

So through my eyes her gesture, pouring in
   On my mind's eye, shaped mine; I stared wide-eyed
   On the sun's face, beyond the wont of men.[5]

It was Beatrice who took Virgil's place as Dante's guide beyond Mount Purgatory through the vast sea of being. Her gesture, which Dante repeats, is literally to gaze upon the sun. There is, however, a metaphorical way in which her gesture shapes Dante's which can be grasped by remembering her promise in the last canto of the *Purgatorio* to use thereafter "a naked style of speech."[6] The promise occurs, suggestively, in the earthly paradise, a restored Eden. The suggestion is that language was to be miraculously restored to its pristine innocence. If with mankind's fall speech itself disintegrated, if language originally meant to unite mankind and all of creation became an instrument of deception and division, concealing rather than revealing, then Beatrice's promise to use a naked style of speech betokened an almost unthinkable restoration of language. When, therefore, Dante mimics Beatrice's gesture, he promises a poetic that is marked by a restored language and a renewed imagination. The vantage point he occupies is beyond that of the spirit who patiently waits in the dark as it is also beyond that of the modern who has despaired of emerging from the labyrinth. In terms of our cave prisoner, imagination's vantage point is outside the cave, where things can be seen in the light of day once one has recovered from the initial blinding worked by the sun.

Dante's claims for the new poetic are truly awesome, and yet they are marked by a profound awareness of the poet's insufficiency:

O power divine, grant me in song to show
   The blest realm's image—shadow though it be—
   Stamped on my brain; thus far thyself bestow.[7]

The poet who takes his cues from Beatrice, staring on the sun's face and seeing everything in its light, who with her is becoming transfigured in the process of fathoming "the love that moves the sun and the other stars," the love that satisfies heart's desire, watches the showers of images he sends forth to display the blinding vision break one by one. In the *Paradiso* images explode in a dazzling shower of sparks and flares that exhilarate the reader who strives to follow Dante on his journey to the center of the stars.

How came Dante to such a lofty position? What seas has he already traversed on his way to the ocean of being? This question brings us back to the beginning of Dante's journey as it also brings us back to the beginning of the pilgrim's journey into the dark. The *Divine Comedy* invites many readings, as a library of commentary has shown. The one offered in the remaining pages is almost exclusively concerned with the inner journey into the soul's dark spaces, a journey we have been making from the beginning of our inquiry.

We join Dante[8] now in the beginning of the *Divine Comedy* awakening to find himself lost "in a dark wood, where the right road was wholly lost and gone."[9] How he came to be there he cannot say, "so heavy and so full of sleep"[10] was he when first he "stumbled from the narrow way."[11] Then he looks up and glimpses the sunlight falling on the side of the mountain before him:

> And this a little quieted the affright
> That lurking in my bosom's lake had lain
> Through the long horror of that piteous night.[12]

Dante here is not unlike the person who, in becoming still, is able to feel the darkness of his origins and his destiny and begins to feel a warm presence that calls him forth into the dark. Dante shared the insight of the mystics that the journey into the dark is sometimes never taken because of the preoccupations crowding into the life on the one hand and the inclination to be fascinated with one's own fancies on the other. Dante is lost, but compared to one who has not glimpsed the morning rays of the sun, he is, as he expresses it himself, like a swimmer who has just reached the shore after crossing through perilous waters. One who is preoccupied, one who is lost in the preoccupations that flood into the life, one who has not awakened, one who characteristically does not raise his eyes and see if only for a moment the rays of the sun, is not even aware of the need for a journey, is not alive to the nature of the quest.

The rare one who has managed to become still, to feel the darkness of his origins and his destiny and who lays aside his preoccupations and his own conceits still faces a long and perilous journey in the night, in the dark. That is why Dante invokes the image of the swimmer who escapes death by water only to confront the desert and its particular perils. Though Dante has escaped something like death by drowning, he faces now a desert that turns out to be the place of the leopard, the lion, and the wolf. These ominous figures inhabit this arid region looking for souls to devour.

Theologically the contrasting images underscore the difference between the conversion that puts one back on the way and the salvation that awaits the faithful. They echo the Exodus story in which the people Israel cross the Red Sea, wherein the Egyptians drown, only to find themselves wandering in the desert. Not everyone called out of Egypt reaches the promised land. The images also echo the writings of the desert fathers, the third- and fourth-century monks who turned their backs on the great affairs of church and state and headed in large numbers into the desert. They had left the battles of the world behind to turn their attention to the battle within their own hearts. As the abbot Antony said, "Who sits in solitude and is quiet hath escaped three wars: hearing, speaking, seeing: yet against one thing shall he continually battle: that is, his own heart."[13] Interestingly enough, the writings of the desert are full of descriptions of disciplines devised to master three vices: lust, anger, and pride or vainglory, vices not badly imaged by leopard, lion, and wolf.

In the *Divine Comedy*, it is as if when Dante first sets out alone on the inner journey in the stillness, in the dark, through the empty spaces of the soul, he almost inevitably encounters resistances to the journey that are so profound that they appear as forces outside himself that he cannot hope to overcome alone. Each image is more ominous than the last, culminating in that of the wolf:

> And next, a Wolf, gaunt with the famished craving
> Lodged ever in her horrible lean flank,
> The ancient cause of many men's enslaving;
> She was the worst—at that dread sight a blank
> Despair and whelming terror pinned me fast,
> Until all hope to scale the mountain sank.
> Like one who loves the gains he has amassed,
> And meets the hour when he must lose his loot,
> Distracted in his mind and all aghast,
> Even so was I, faced with that restless brute
> Which little by little edged and thrust me back,
> Back to that place wherein the sun is mute.[14]

Although the innermost meaning of the image of the wolf awaits disclosure in the last circle of hell, there is no missing here the depth of despair the wolf occasions in Dante. The sun is mute. On his own, Dante is powerless, hurled back toward the wood from which he has recently emerged. He almost fails to notice grace's emissary, Virgil, and the power of poetry and images he represents. If despair is the final fate of the self-reliant, the vainglorious, those who pridefully rely on their own power to save their lives and to give life meaning, then Dante's recognition of Virgil and his acceptance of him as his guide, insignificant as it may first appear, is crucial for the journey through and beyond despair. The poet's description of Dante's recognition of Virgil is so striking that it is easy to miss the significance of the spiritual motion in Dante when he sets aside reliance on his own powers to

take him through the wasteland and instead accepts Virgil as his
guide. It is the one act that decisively distinguishes Dante from
the damned. The almost imperceptible movement of his spirit in
accepting Virgil as his guide undermines the vainglory that is the
underside of despair. The resistance the wolf represents—the
despair that keeps a soul from journeying through the dark—is a
resistance that is dealt with only by going with a guide through
the places where there is no hope, no light of day. Virgil takes
Dante, then, not away from hell's emissary, but right into its
jaws. Dorothy Sayers is right when she comments that, once lost
in a dark wood, a man can escape only by so descending into
himself that he sees his sin, not as an external obstacle, but as the
will to chaos and death within him; only when he has died to sin
can he repent and purge it.[15] If it is despair that threatens to
devour Dante, it is fitting that he go the way trod by those who
have laid down all hope. The path by which Virgil takes him
through the portals of hell is not then a movement away from the
wolf but a movement through its jaws and into its bowels. The
move whereby Dante puts his trust in another sets in motion a dy-
namic whereby Dante finally moves beyond despair.[16] His descent
into hell takes place Good Friday evening.

    There are many things that might be noted about the
images the poet places before the reader as Dante explores with
Virgil's assistance the depths of despair. One learns a great deal
simply by paying attention to the geography of the journey. The
circular movement of the journey, for example, calls attention to
the importance of circles generally to the story and invites a contrast between the vicious circles of hell from which there is no
release, the spiralling circles of Mount Purgatory—circles of suffering that has a point—and finally the heavenly spheres whose
divine center is everywhere and whose circumference is nowhere.
From the vicious circles of selves who insist on being the center of
their worlds, through the spiralling circles of selves learning to let
go the impulse to remain at the center, to the spheres where God

is at the center of lives that move in the freedom of his love, the *Divine Comedy* progresses.

There is one feature common to the images of the punishments of the damned that we will wish to stress in the pages that follow. In every instance the picture of the penalty discloses the image which, in time, the sinner allowed to hold his life. A simple exercise will illumine the meaning of an image that holds a life. Suppose we draw on a blank piece of paper five circles, like this:

Suppose in each of the circles we place an image that says a great deal about who we are. Suppose then we ask ourselves if we would be willing to let go the images we think define us. As we learn which images we are most loath to give up, we discover that they converge on a central image that holds us like a vessel. The image that holds the life would be like that image, the image we clutch close to us and refuse to let go of. Sin, then, would be letting something less than God hold the life. When the effective will of the God who wills men to choose freely who they shall be ratifies the sinner's choice, the life is fixed eternally in a vicious circle whose center is the self.

What Dante glimpses in his vision of hell are images that hold the lives of the damned, images that are frozen now in the punishments that merely crystallized their life choices—images that *could* hold Dante. What before Dante encountered as fearful obstacles to the journey through the desert places appear now as deliberate movements of souls away from God, beginning with the almost innocent adultery of Paolo and Francesca, but moving with the full weight of gravity to the unspeakable treachery of Judas. The movement from the kiss of Paolo and Francesca to the kiss of Judas charts the progress from the apparent innocence of adultery—the first sign of faithlessness and the Hebrew prototype for sin—to the evident malice of betrayal—the deliberate rejection of the heart's desire.

The vision in the last circle of hell illumining the innermost meaning of the despair that is at the bottom of the soul's resistance to the journey to God is chilling. Dante arrives with Virgil at the region of ice, "where at last the shades, quite covered by the frozen sheet, gleamed through the ice like straws in crystal glassed."[17] Dante looks on in horror: "This was not life, and yet it was not death."[18]

Out of the ice rose Satan. In him God's image is hideously perverted: three faces make up the Satanhead. His six eyes weep their rage. Each mouth gnaws a sinner, a traitor. Virgil identifies the souls eternally devoured by Hell's emperor:

"That wretch up there whom keenest pangs divide
    Is Judas called Iscariot," said my lord,
    "His head within, his jerking legs outside;
As for the pair whose heads hang hitherward;
    From the black mouth the limbs of Brutus sprawl—
    See how he writhes and utters never a word;
And strong-thewed Cassius is his fellow-thrall.
    But come; for night is rising on the world
    Once more; we must depart; we have seen all."[19]

At last Dante beholds the true meaning of his deepest resistance to the journey to God, a resistance that first he felt as fear when he beheld the wolf. The roots of despair are exposed in the image of Satan feeding on the souls of Judas, Brutus, and Cassius. Satan, the hungry wolf, prowls eternally in search of souls to devour in order to satisfy an insatiable appetite, the infinite emptiness that defines him when he deliberately and pridefully turns away from God, who alone can satisfy the heart's desire. Dante sees for the first time that resistance to the journey to God is rooted in vanity, a vainglorious rejection of what is freely offered. Despair finally appears as the most damnable form of treachery, the soul's gift to the devil. For in turning aside from the God who would draw all to himself, the soul reveals its preference to be devoured by, and so be joined in spirit to, the one who first and finally broke from God. In one master stroke the poet shows what it would be to let the wolf turn one away from the journey. The picture of the traitors becoming food for Satan discloses the kind of pact one enters into when one refuses to respond to God's call. The image of Satan reveals the full dimensions of a deliberate vainglorious refusal of what God freely offers.

As Dante moves through the ice with Virgil first down and then up Satan's shaggy flanks, Dante is bewildered:

> I raised my eyes, thinking to see the top
> > Of Lucifer, as I had left him last,
> > But only saw his great legs sticking up.[20]

He asks Virgil to explain what has happened to the ice and "what's turned him upside down?"[21] Virgil explains that in passing through the center of hell they passed through the center of the earth and are now in the Southern Hemisphere so that "up" and "down" are reversed.[22] It would be just as reasonable to say that it is Dante who is turned upside down. They follow a small stream "back to the lit world from the darkened dens."[23]

Dante has emerged from the soul's dark night, through the desert where temptations are experienced as resistances to the spiritual journey. The almost imperceptible movement by which Dante accepted Virgil as his guide, letting go the impulse to be the master of his destiny, culminates in Dante's movement through the pit of despair to "look once more upon the stars."[24] That movement through the last circle of hell, when the whole of his world seemed suddenly to be turned upside down, marks a conversion far more radical than Dante's earlier awakening. Yet Dante emerges only to confront Mount Purgatory and the more time-consuming task of letting go the images that hold the life in vicious circles and accepting in their place the images that free the soul to advance on the journey to God. Dante has uncovered at a

step removed, in the images of *others'* eternal choices, the roots of
sin, of turning from God. He has yet to recognize the precise
character of his own betrayal and to repent it. If he has beheld a
heart frozen in its resistance to God, heavy with despair, he has
yet to have his own heart broken, that it might one day be light
as the hearts of those who are filled with love of God.

Earlier we proposed an exercise to better understand what it
means for an image to hold the life. If we continue with that exercise, we can understand more clearly what it would mean for an
image to free the life. If, for example, we were to let an image
that we recognize as the dominant image from a Scriptural passage we are reading stand in the place of one of the images we
have already recognized as in a way defining us, and if we were
willing to let the new image inform our living, we would come to
know how the heart can be transformed, how the life can be
freed. It would be important that the image we put in place of
the old be from a source other than ourselves. If it were an image
we simply conjured up, we would, in effect, merely be filling the
void with imagination. We would not really be open to a truly
radical transformation. Nor would it be wise to carry out such an
exercise without the guidance of a master of the spiritual life, lest
we do violence to the source we turn to and our own selves.
Despite these precautionary remarks, the notions of letting go the
images that hold the life in vicious circles and accepting in their
place the images that free the life are useful notions for understanding the general significance of the *Purgatorio* and for grasping the significance of Beatrice both for the pilgrim and for the
poet. It would be difficult otherwise to fathom how Beatrice is
both the instrument of Dante's salvation and the sine qua non of
the poet's breakthrough. Hence we will regard Dante's journey
up Mount Purgatory as a journey in the course of which he learns
to let go the images that held his life and in their place accept—
well, the image of Beatrice.

As in the *Inferno* Dante awoke to find himself lost in a dark wood, in the ninth canto of the *Purgatorio* Dante awakens from a dream in which an eagle "caught me up into the sphere of flame."[25] He discovers that he has in fact been carried by a lady from heaven to Saint Peter's Gate, the entrance to Purgatory proper, the first of many fissures through circular walls. Again Dante "stared and started and felt lost."[26]

Before he is permitted by God's Angel to pass through the Gate, he must mount three steps:

> And when we reached the first step of the stair
> > It was white marble, polished to such gloss
> > That, even as I am, I saw me there;
> And dyed more dark than perse the second was—
> > A calcined stone, rugged and rough in grain,
> > And it was cracked both lengthways and across;
> The third step, piled above the other twain,
> > Seemed all of porphyry that flamed and shone
> > Redder than bright blood spurting from a vein.[27]

Dorothy Sayers' gloss is to the point:

> These are the three parts of Penitence: (1) Confession, (2) Contrition, (3) Satisfaction. The first is of polished white marble: the penitent looks into his heart, sees himself as he is, recognizes his sinfulness, and so admits and confesses it. The second is black, the colour of mourning, and cracked in the figure of the cross: "A broken and contrite heart, O God, shalt thou not despise" (*Ps.* li. 17, *Vulg.* i. 19). The third is of porphyry redder than blood: the colour symbolizes not only the penitent's pouring out of his own life and love in restitution for sin, but also the Blood of Christ's "oblation of Himself and offered, to be a full, perfect and sufficient sacrifice, oblation, and satisfaction for the sins of the whole world" (*Book of Common Prayer*), with which the penitent's satisfaction must unite itself in order to be complete.[28]

The steps prefigure Dante's movement through the rest of the *Purgatorio*, for though he mounts the steps to receive from the sword point of the Angel the mark of seven P's upon his brow

and then passes through the gate, he more truly mounts those
steps much later in the *Purgatorio* when he experiences what each
step signifies. In other words, the steps are symbolic in the ninth
canto, and his mounting them is symbolic here, too. The symbol
is realized much later as, step by step, Dante's heart is purified,
crushed, and opened.

As the ninth canto prefigures in symbol an experience yet to
be undergone (not unlike the first canto of the *Inferno* in this
regard), cantos ten through twenty-six elaborate what is involved
in *realizing* the symbol by revealing to Dante the nature of purga-
torial suffering in the images of *others'* suffering (not unlike the
development of the *Inferno* in this regard). Significantly different
from the *Inferno*, however, is the conclusion of the *Purgatorio*,
where Dante actually experiences himself what has been first
symbolized and then illumined in the images of others' suffering.
It had to be so, for Dante is not one of the damned.

As in the circles of Hell, the punishments that Dante beholds on the terraces of Mount Purgatory reveal the images that
held the soul in life and threaten to fix it in eternity. What distinguishes the *Purgatorio* from the *Inferno*, however, is the presence on every terrace of an image counter to the image that holds
the soul back from making any progress on the journey to God.
The counter-image is actually a double-image: a portrait from the
life of the Virgin Mary and a saving gesture from the life of the
suffering soul which shows a break in the image that would
otherwise have confined the life in a vicious circle. What Dante
sees on the first cornice, the cornice wherein the proud are
cleansed, is illustrative. Even before Dante observes the suffering
of the proud he sees carved in pure white marble a sculpture of
the Annunciation:

> And in her mien those words stood plain to see:
> > *Ecce ancilla Dei*, stamped by art
> > Express as any seal on wax could be.[29]

In one stroke is imaged God's humility in deigning to become man and Mary's in accepting the divine burden. On the same terrace Dante hears of Provenzan Salvani, whose arrogance was notorious and whom Dante would have expected to find among the damned. What he hears shows a crack in the image of arrogance, the crack through which Provenzan will eventually emerge into Paradise:

> In mid-splendour of his course
> > He in Siena's market went and stood,
> > Of his free-will, all shame thrown out of doors;
> And, to redeem his friend from servitude
> > In Charles' dungeon, there he bore to do
> > A thing he winced at in his very blood.[30]

For love of his friend, Provenzan stooped to beg in the market at the height of his splendour, showing that the arrogance which in other ways held him back from spiritual advance, in one self-revealing moment gave way to a power that was greater. In Dante's words, "That deed undid the ban and set him free."[31]

What Dante learns as he ascends from cornice to cornice is that the repentant sinner must let go the image that holds the life and in its place allow the image that frees it. But for all that he learns and even though he has each of the seven P's wiped away as he ascends, Dante does not himself actually experience what was prefigured in the steps and elaborated in the images of repentance until he himself passes through the fire in the twenty-seventh canto.[32]

Of that cleansing fire a number of things need to be said. Since the earthly paradise lies the other side of it, the fire is on one level the flaming sword of the angel left there to prevent sinful man from reentering the garden and eating from the tree of life. Hence it is through this fire that everyman must pass who has fallen in Adam.

But there is another way in which Dante, who is in figure

everyman, most fittingly endures this fire. We remember that in the *Inferno* the first image we are given of the faithlessness that is at the bottom of Dante's departure from the right path is the adulterous kiss of Paolo and Francesca. In the Hebrew Scriptures, adultery is the prototype for sin, since for the Hebrew sin in its most fundamental reality is the faithless violation of their covenant with God. While the Hebrews regarded such sin as the act and responsibility of a people, Dante, following Christian precedents, sees adultery, faithlessness, as the act and responsibility of the individual who willfully turns away from God, choosing rather to be at the center of a vicious circle. Dante suggests that his sin—but, of course, that is everyman's sin, or the way original sin is actualized in everyone—consists in putting something less than God where God belongs, in giving himself to something or someone less than the one who alone can satisfy the heart's desire. Sin, then, is fundamentally love gone crazy, a fact that helps one better understand the force of the demonic powers and the dimensions of the upheaval occasioned by Satan's fall which Dante images in the geographical dislocations described above.[33] The poet's prism breaks the fundamental sin into its separate parts in the *Inferno*, providing a phenomenology of sin not likely to be surpassed. The movement away from God from the first subtle straying to the final rejection is one anyone can recognize yet few could describe.

If fire is an image of passion, of love gone crazy, it is also an image of purification and tempering, of love redeemed. One could scarcely find a better image by which to display Dante's— and everyman's—sin. But what of the counter-image? We have come to expect one in the preceding cantos. Nor are we disappointed. As Dante endures the fire, which he describes so:

And I, being in, would have been glad to throw
    Myself for coolness into molten glass,
    With such unmeasured heat did that fire glow.[34]

he is sustained by the image of Beatrice:

> My gentle father (Virgil) talked to cheer me—'twas
> Beatrice all the way: "Methinks even now
> Her eyes," he'd say, "shine to me through the pass."[35]

Dante here begins to experience what he had in symbol done
before when he mounted the first step at Saint Peter's Gate. He
begins to experience what it is to be pure of heart. The angel who
greeted Dante through the flames had sung *"Beati mundo corde"*
—"Blessed are the pure in heart."[36] The tempering of Dante's
spirit consists in letting go the images he had put in place of Beatrice and accepting her image instead. As anyone knows who has
let an image from the Scriptures challenge an image that he has
allowed in its place, the very presence of the proper image accuses
him. When in the thirtieth canto Dante actually encounters Beatrice, she says:

> Look on us well; we are indeed, we are
> Beatrice . . .[37]

Dante now begins to feel the full force of the old love, and its
double edge amplifies the poet's earlier image of the tempering
fire:

> I dropped my eyes down to the glassy rill,
> Saw myself there, and quickly to the brink
> Withdrew them, bowed with shame unspeakable.[38]

When Beatrice's court ask Beatrice why she puts him so to
shame, she replies:

> That he who yonder weeps should comprehend,
> And grief with guilt maintain the balance true.[39]

Then she confronts Dante with his particular sin:

> I with my countenance some time indeed
> Upheld him; my young eyes his beacon were
> To turn him right and in my steps to lead;

But when I'd reached my second age, and then,
    E'en on the threshold, life for life exchanged,
    Then he forsook me and made friends elsewhere.

. . .

    His mind was turned from me, his heart estranged;
And by wild ways he wandered . . .
    . . .

With inspirations . . .
    Vainly in dreams . . .
    I called him home
And in the end, to such a depth he fell
    That every means to save his soul came short
    Except to let him see the lost in hell.

. . .

It would do violence to God's high doom
    If Lethe could be passed, and ill-doers
    To taste this blessed fare could straightway come
Without some forfeit of repentant tears.[40]

Still Dante has not fully mounted that first step. The images of
the old man and the new clash in Dante's heart. To accept Beatrice in place of her surrogates, to let himself be formed anew in
her image, meant first of all to admit the truth of her accusation.
She pressed him:

"Say, say if this is true; so grave a charge
    Requires thine own confession; therefore say."

. . .

"Answer me; thy sad memories are not yet
    Drowned by this water of oblivion."[41]

At last he rests on that first step of confession:

Terror and shame inextricably knit
    Forced from my miserable lips a "Yes."[42]

Almost immediately he advances to the second: "I broke beneath
the weight of this assault . . ."[43] If earlier Dante's symbolic
mounting of the steps happened with some dispatch, the progress

here is somewhat more drawn out. Dante may have broken with his confession, but Beatrice does not stop her assault. She means to pulverize and crush him. The step one mounts in becoming contrite, of having one's heart literally crushed, means that there is no return to the old life. The old image that once held the life in a vicious circle must be shattered beyond repair. God help the soul who is so shattered but for whom there is no Beatrice!

The meaning of Beatrice begins in these cantos to emerge. She arrives in a car drawn by a Gryphon in a pageant reminiscent of the Corpus Christi processions. She confronts Dante with his sin, eliciting his confession and his contrition. Now she bids him hold up his beard and endure yet greater grief. What greater grief is there to endure? Already Dante has seen himself in his faithlessness. Already Dante has been crushed. What greater grief is this of which Beatrice speaks?

Again we recall Dorothy Sayers' gloss of the third step the penitent mounts, the step Dante has yet to take:

> The third is of porphyry redder than blood: the colour symbolizes not only the penitent's pouring out of his own life and love in restitution for sin, but also the Blood of Christ's "oblation of Himself once offered, to be a full, perfect and sufficient sacrifice, oblation, and satisfaction for the sins of the whole world" (*Book of Common Prayer*), with which the penitent's satisfaction must unite itself in order to be complete.[44]

What Sayers here describes could hardly be better imaged than in the act of the penitent's receiving communion, letting his own life-blood pour into and mingle with the life-blood shed for all mankind. When the poet has Dante stretch his neck erect to behold Beatrice turned toward the Gryphon ("to him that is one person sole in natures two"[45]), he deliberately refers us at one level to that act of communion. But he immediately endows the act with all that his poetic genius can muster:

> And there, beneath her veil, beyond the stream,

> Her former self, methought, she more outshone
> > Than here, with others, she once outshone them.
> Such nettles of remorse stung me thereon
> > That of all other objects of my love
> > I hated most what I'd most doted on;
> And gnawing self-reproach my heart so clove,
> > I swooned and sank . . .[46]

What Dante beholds when he sees Beatrice unveiled—which causes him yet greater grief—provokes him to let go finally the last hold on the images that once had endeared him (even the image of Beatrice when she was just a pretty girl to him). He pours out his own life and love, he swoons and sinks. He finds himself in the river Lethe held by Lucy:

> Into the stream she'd drawn me in my faint,
> > Throat-high, and now, towing me after her,
> > Light as a shuttle o'er the water went.
>
>   . . .
>
> She stretched both hands, she seized me by the crown,
> > Did that fair lady, and she plunged me in,
> > So that I needs must drink the water down:[47]

Beatrice's handmaids lead him then to Beatrice, to gaze into her green eyes:

> Myriad desires, hotter than fire or scald
> > Fastened mine eyes upon the shining eyes
> > That from the Gryphon never loosed their hold.
> Like sun in looking-glass, no otherwise,
> > I saw the Twyform mirrored in their range,
> > Now in the one, now in the other guise
> Think, Reader, think how marvelous and strange
> > It seemed to me when I beheld the thing
> > Itself stand changeless and the image change.[48]

The full meaning of what Dante beholds that brings him yet greater grief yet also elicits his life gift is at last made clear. When Dante first raised his beard he beheld for the first time Beatrice unveiled—looking toward the Gryphon. These last three stanzas fill out the vision that inform the eyes of Beatrice. In between we are given the image of Dante's swoon wherein he pours himself out, forgetting forever his former self, surrounded by and giving substance to the images of baptism and communion. What Dante beholds when he sees Beatrice unveiled is something eminently natural and yet absolutely incomprehensible: eyes that offer the one thing that could bring him to yet greater grief and yet elicit his life-gift: the forgiving love that is at once the most human gift one person can bestow upon another and yet, in this instance, the strange and marvelous gift that removes from Dante's memory every trace of his treachery and his remorse.

The poet strains to express in image what no image can begin to match in beauty for one who has betrayed another and who, beyond reasonable hope, finds himself forgiven. The poet invokes the most sacrosanct of Christian symbols, the sacraments of baptism and communion, portrays Beatrice as gazing on the Gryphon (one person sole in natures two), as if her eyes are informed by what the Gryphon represents, a love at once most human and yet more than human; yet the reader realizes that not even these attempts of sheer poetic genius can quite measure what they intend. Yet Dante must make every effort to record the vision that fills and forms the eyes that return his gaze when he looks up, for it is a vision Virgil never knew. It founds a new poetic. The thirty-first canto ends with Beatrice's handmaids entreating her to reveal her mouth to him, "that he may discern the second beauty which thou dost conceal."[49] In effect they are asking Beatrice to tell what it is that informs her eyes, the eyes whose love frees Dante from every memory of transgression. In the thirty-second canto the poet offers not Beatrice's words but another dazzling poetic attempt to shadow them. There unfolds a pageant. The Gryphon once again leads the heavenly car forward and the march resumes through the earthly paradise:

> Haply we had advanced about as far
> As three flights of an arrow might have spanned,
> When Beatrix descended from the car.

I heard all murmur "Adam": then their stand
  They took beneath a tree whose boughs were shred
  Bare of all flowers and leaves on every hand.

The more it rose, the wider still it spread,
  And Indians in their woods it well might fill
  With wonder to behold its lofty head.

"Blessed art thou, O Gryphon, that thy bill
  Plucks nothing from this tree of sweetest gust,
  Which wrung the belly with such griping ill."

Thus cried they all, circling the trunk august.
  Then spake the Beast in whom two natures met:
  "Thus is preserved the seed of all that's just."

And turning to the pole he'd drawn, he set
  His strength to drag it to the widowed tree,
  And what came from it he left bound to it.[50]

So the beast fixes the chariot pole to the tree through which
death came into the world and

Brighter than violets, deeper than the rose,
  Suffused with colour, fresh and green it grew,
  The tree that was so bare in all its boughs.[51]

According to legend, the wood of the cross was from the tree of
the knowledge of good and evil of whose fruit Adam ate, bringing death to all men. In figure, the Gryphon in restoring the
wood to the tree, restores life to the tree and so "preserves the
seed of all that's just."[52]

It is the vision of Christ's act of laying down his life for
those he loved, the consummate act of God's forgiveness and love,
majestically and stylistically presented here in the pageant, that
filled Beatrice's eyes with what Virgil never knew. Were there no
Christ who lay down his life on the cross, revealing the lengths he
was prepared to go to change the hearts of those who betrayed his
love, there would be no such eyes to save Dante from destruction.
Persons who have known love and forgiveness can offer them to
another. If the pagan could achieve purity of heart and in some

way comprehend contrition, the pagan could in no way comprehend the kind of love that could erase from memory the despair and remorse of the sinner.

Dante, newly restored to innocence—as much by bathing in the eyes of Beatrice as in the waters of Lethe—is at a loss to express the vision that opens out to him, despite Beatrice's promise to "use a naked style of speech,"[53] speech that reveals rather than conceals. He must now enter the stream of Eunoe. It is almost as if he must learn a new language founded upon a new memory if he is to begin to communicate that vision. The *Paradiso*, then, may be regarded as Dante's attempt to fathom the love that erases the memory of sin, that fills the void, that raises one who has died. Each sphere to which Dante ecstatically ascends contains another image of the love that both moves Beatrice and is embodied in her.

With the movement to the *Paradiso*, Dante also embarks on poetic waters yet undared. As Beatrice is the instrument of Dante's salvation, she is also the key to the new poetic. The poet forcefully impresses upon the reader that it is in the eyes of Beatrice that Dante discovers the fullness of the Christian mysteries. Were those eyes not there, the Christian vision would evaporate. The pilgrim would languish in the wood. But we should also note that the poet would produce no *Divine Comedy*. In a world of so many faces and facades, those eyes are astonishing and hold the poet's attention. His attempt to find words to express aptly his astonishment is displayed in the magnificent vision of the Gryphon that the pageant elaborates. But the poet does not want us to detach the vision from its embodiment, to get lost in the edifying poetic and theological vision, but rather to be reminded that in our very real world of faces and facades there are astonishing eyes that should hold our attention and that ground those visions. Even as he has Dante cross the stream of Eunoe, the poet would have his reader "remember well," that is, be mindful of the astonishing reality of things lest they fall away into the faded, undifferentiated tangle of the everyday.

Dante's journey to God parallels the poet's advance to a new poetic. As the pilgrim learns to be freed from the images that hold him in vicious circles and to embrace the images that open the way to God, the poet learns to let go the impulse to fill the void with imagination and rather to take his bearings from realities not of his own invention. As progress in the inner journey involves a painful confrontation with one's own betrayals, a complete and utter confession of and rejection of the lie one is living —in short, a death and rebirth—so progress in the new poetic involves a similar cleansing, a refusal to be impressed with one's own poetic brilliance, with the images and fictions one can conjure up or contrive, and a willingness to let the art itself be subordinate to the realities that offer it one challenge greater than another and invite the poet to approach anew the threshold of awe. Appropriately, as Dante embarks with Beatrice upon the Ocean of *being*, he issues a stern warning to anyone whose predisposition is merely to "follow . . . for the song's sake,"[54] for such a one would never reach the port the poet intends. When he adds

> But you, rare souls, that have reached up to seize
>> Betimes the bread of angels, food for men
>> To live on here, whereof no surfeit is,
> You may commit your bark unto the main.[55]

he reminds the reader of the act of self-donation at the end of the *Purgatorio* which, in completing the pilgrim's purging, prepared him for his entrance into Paradise. But with these words he is also, as poet, letting his poetry be shaped by real events, simply recalling his reader to the words spoken in the Offertory to the Mass of the day in which Dante's ascent through the heavenly spheres figuratively takes place:

> The Lord opened the doors of heaven: and he rained down on them manna that they might eat: he gave them the bread of heaven: the bread of angels has man eaten, alleluja.[56]

Before embarking with Dante on his journey through the Ocean of being, let us recall very briefly the way we have come. At the outset we were with Dante lost in a dark wood; we felt with him the darkness that surrounded his origins and his destiny. We beheld him appalled at the desolateness, the emptiness of his own soul. We saw in him the resistance to the journey in the dark to the one whose love alone could fill the void, whose love reached out to him in his desolation. First felt as despair, that resistance was revealed as rooted in a vainglorious rejection of God, a preference for one's own empty self, and appeared finally as a howling, unsatisfied desire. Dante managed to make his way through the desert of despair by accepting Virgil as a guide. Dante's acceptance of Virgil, it seems in retrospect, saved him from the pit of self-love. Yet not even Virgil could secure for him bliss, salvation from his own emptiness, satisfaction of his heart's desire. What matters most about Beatrice is that she, like Virgil, could never have been conjured up. As the sinner, the traitor, cannot on his own summon up the love and forgiveness that alone can save him, the poet cannot bring into being what his words and images so poorly shadow. Dante, pilgrim and poet, is saved from his own vanity the moment his attention is held by those eyes that elicit his life-gift.

Dante's movement through the *Paradiso*, then, might best be understood as the poet's attempt to filter through his poetic prism the love that fills the void. It is no abstract love, but real love embodied in Beatrice that holds Dante's attention. Dante's journey, now perceived as a journey to God, proceeds as Dante accepts all that Beatrice represents in place of everything that he had in the past put in her place. He lets his own life become informed with her reality, a reality he fathoms further and further as he is led in ecstasy outside and beyond himself. The journey culminates, as we shall soon see, in a vision of the mystery of the Incarnation, of the God made flesh, the divine embodiment that renders blessed all the realities that point to it.

The poet, in passing sin through his poetic prism, offered a phenomenology of sin without compare by subtly tracing the soul's movement from the first, nearly imperceptible infidelity to the patent treachery of love's rejection. Now the poet offers a phenomenology of love by tracing the movements of the soul whose initial fidelity opens on to love's fulfillment. Throughout the *Paradiso* God's love is reflected in the love embodied in real persons and in the gestures of real persons. Hence in fathoming that love that moves Beatrice, it is fitting that Dante recognize love's movements as they are reflected in the lives of the blessed.

He meets, for example, Justinian,

"Who from the laws—urged by that Primal Love
    Which I now feel—winnowed the dust and bran."[57]

He meets Cunizza, the colorful Florentine lady who passed her old age in the performance of acts of mercy and compassion. She says, "I glitter here because I was o'ermastered by this planet's (Venus') flame."[58] He meets Thomas Aquinas, who says:

"Lamb of the holy flock was I, obeying
    Dominic on that road he led us by,
    Where is good fattening if there be no straying."[59]

Justinian accounts for the source of all their joy:

"The Light whose radiance runs through all the spheres
    Illumines us . . . ."[60]

Throughout the Ocean of being God's love is pervasive. It meets people wherever they are and is indirectly revealed in the unique life-gestures of the saints. The effect the poet produces is not unlike that produced by the dramatist of *Godspell*, who has Jesus take leave of his disciples one by one, offering to each the gesture which the audience has come to identify with each. Each disciple recognizes himself in the gesture; each recognizes himself as uniquely loved and affirmed in the gesture; no one would want another's gesture returned to him on this occasion. The poet of the

Divine Comedy achieves the same effect by having Dante ascend from sphere to sphere, beholding the gestures that eternally opened the lives of the saved to God. No one envies anyone else's place in the heavenly dispensation. Yet in each life, imaged in a unique gesture, there is present another image of the love that first sought it out. Piccarda dei Donati explains:

> "Brother, our love has laid our wills to rest,
>> Making us long only for what is ours,
>> And by no other thirst to be possessed.
>
> . . .
>
> . . . and His will is our peace."[61]

The poet recognizes that love is not properly split up in the manner he is compelled to adopt in the *Divine Comedy*. Hence in the last canto he brings back together in the figure of the celestial rose what he has sundered poetically along the way. St. Bernard guides Dante's gaze amid the petals of the rose:

> The wound which Mary tended and assuaged
>> Was by the beauteous person at her feet
>> Inflicted in surrender so ill-gauged.
> Among the thrones of the third order sit,
>> Below her, Rachel, and, as thou canst see,
>> Thy Beatrice in the adjacent seat.
> Sara, Rebekah, Judith and then she,
>> The ancestress of him who cried in grief
>> At his wrong doing, *Miserere mei,*
> Throne after throne, will greet thy vision if
>> It keep with me as, naming them, I go
>> Down through the rose, proceeding leaf by leaf.[62]

Bernard explains that

> Since faith from two directions turned her gaze
>> To Christ, these holy women form the wall
>> Which indicates the parting of the ways.[63]

So the rose incorporates the witness to Christ of Old and New Testaments. The design of the rose is divinely ordained:

For here eternal law doth so enact
>All thou beholdest, that the measurements
>Between the ring and finger are exact.

Swift-sped to the true life, this child-folk, hence,
>Not *sine causa* in this Rose reside
>In varying degrees of excellence.

The King, within whose kingdom we abide
>Content in love and blissfulness so great
>No will has dared to long for more beside,

All minds in His glad semblance doth create;
>His grace thereon is variously conferred.
>Thou seest the effect; let that be adequate.[64]

Finally, Bernard entreats Mary the heavenly Queen to grant Dante

. . . such might
>That higher yet in vision he may rise
>Towards the final source of bliss and light.[65]

Dante looks upward, anticipating Bernard's cue:

Henceforth my vision mounted to a height
>Where speech is vanquished and must lag behind,
>And memory surrenders in such plight.

As from a dream one may awake to find
>Its passion yet imprinted on the heart,
>Although all else is cancelled from the mind,

So of my vision now but little part
>Remains, yet in my inmost soul I know
>The sweet instilling which it did impart.[66]

Before going on, Dante prays that in his words may burn "one single spark of all Thy glory's light."[67] Of that vision he sings:

O grace abounding, whereby I presumed
>So deep the eternal light to search and sound
>That my whole vision was therein consumed!

In that abyss I saw how love held bound
>Into one volume all the leaves whose flight

Is scattered through the universe around;

. . .

And so my mind, bedazzled and amazed,
 Stood fixed in wonder, motionless, intent,
 And still my wonder kindled as I gazed.
That light doth so transform a man's whole bent
 That never to another sight or thought
 Would he surrender, with his own consent;
For everything the will has ever sought
 Is gathered there, and there is every quest
 Made perfect, which apart from it falls short.[68]

Had Dante's vision ended here, the poet would have composed another poem, if indeed he would have composed at all, for it seems that all divisions cease in the end and all images dissolve. There would be nothing with which to compose. But Dante goes on to say:

But as my sight by seeing learned to see,
 The transformation which in me took place
 Transformed the single changeless form for me.
That light supreme, within its fathomless
 Clear substance, showed to me three spheres, which
  bare
 Three hues distinct, and occupied one space;
The first mirrored the next, as though it were
 Rainbow from rainbow, and the third seemed flame
 Breathed equally from each of the first pair.

. . .

The sphering thus begot, perceptible
 In Thee like mirrored light, now to my view—
 When I had looked on it a little while—
Seemed in itself, and in its own self-hue,
 Limned with our image; for which cause mine eyes
 Were altogether drawn and held thereto.[69]

Dante is amazed:

So strove I with that wonder—how to fit

The image to the sphere; so sought to see
How it maintained the point of the rest in it.
Thither my own wings could not carry me,
But that a flash my understanding clove,
Whence its desire came to it suddenly.
High fantasy lost power and here broke off;
Yet, as a wheel moves smoothly, free from jars,
My will and my desire were turned by love,
The love that moves the sun and the other stars.[70]

Dante never claims to comprehend the flash that clove his understanding, but he cannot doubt that the transformation love works in him, in which his will and desire are turned now "as a wheel . . . free from jars,"[71] is an experience of the reality of the Incarnation, the uniquely Christian experience that grounds, finally, the affirmation of images. At last we reach the heart of the poet's blazing confidence in the intelligibility of images and gestures that embody what the spirit intends. We know finally why we never doubted that Beatrice, most astonishing image of them all, both embodied and pointed to the love that fills the universe and reaches into the darkest regions of the heart.

As anything real points to the power that holds it in existence and keeps it from falling away into nothingness, a poetic that is founded on, takes its bearings from, realities not of its creation derives its power ultimately from the same source. Its words are not hollow utterances of hollow men but embodiments of realities that hold our attention and remind us that in a world of faces and facades there are real thresholds over which we bodily creatures can cross on our journey to God. As C. S. Lewis once remarked, when we are lost in a wood, when first we see a signpost, we shout Look! For that is an event. Something has happened that is not commonplace. But signposts are obscure when we are in the wood, and oddly it is not until we have really become still that we have any hope of discovering them. Like the monarch butterfly that climbs the hill by falling still, it is not until we fall still before an other that the wind that blows through all of us can carry us.

The vantage point of sanctified imagination is markedly different from those we have considered earlier. Even as the pilgrim has had to learn to let go the images that hold the life and embrace in place of them the images that free the life, so the poet has had to learn to refrain from filling the void with imagination, from conjuring up images and stories that, though they might entertain one, finally leave one hollow and hungry for nourishment that is more substantial. The poet who, like Augustine, has fallen still and has become present to the things and events of his life suddenly realizes that among all the faces and facades are those eyes that hold his attention. In all the tangle of life there are presences that point beyond themselves, issuing an invitation to pass through them to the very center of their being. Whereas Augustine, having come to this pass, composed a story that remained throughout faithful to the shape of his life and so intended to display the action of God in his life, Dante turned his gaze outward. Without losing sight of the precise way in which his Lord reached into his life, he turned his gaze outward to discover grace's movements in other lives, in other places. It is in this spirit, in the confidence that the things and events of life are testaments of abounding grace, that Dante approaches his poetic task. So, for example, he finds in the liturgy *actually going on in his day* not just a prop, a convenient structural device, but a *source* for his poetry. When in the second canto Dante says

> But you, rare souls, that have reached up to seize
>   Betimes the bread of angels, food for men
>   To live on here, whereof no surfeit is,
> You may commit your bark to the main.[72]

he is not simply differentiating his epic poem from the lighter lyric poetry of his day as some critics suggest. He is *displaying* rather than saying what is different about his poetry. These words which combine to form an image are words that the poet has willingly and deliberately *received* from the liturgy of his day; they did not spring from out of his own poetic genius. This particularly important instance of this poet's art—important because the poet is directly addressing the reader and instructing him how to read thereafter, if not before—is typical of Dante's practice in the *Divine Comedy*. We have already noted certain liturgical features that importantly shape the poem. The descent into hell begins Good Friday evening. Dante rises out of hell Easter Sunday morning. His own experience of repentance and forgiveness is magnificently portrayed in terms of the pageant of Beatrice, where the incorporation of baptismal and eucharistic images is all the more striking when one recalls that in Dante's day the sacraments of baptism and the eucharist were normally received by the faithful *only* during the Easter season. Not only were those souls rare indeed who "reached up to seize betimes the bread of angels."[73] Those who approached the sacrament in Dante's day had a year to consider the religious seriousness of that event. The ascent to the heavenly spheres, as we have noted, takes place the Wednesday following Easter, the day whose Offertory prayer announces that the Lord has opened the gates of heaven. Finally, the experience of God not just entering into man but entering into Dante as his will and desire were conformed at last to God's takes place exactly twenty-four hours later. In other words, the pilgrim's journeying spans seven days, the number venerated in the Middle Ages because, among other reasons, it was the combination of four and three, numbers themselves suggesting the sphere and square which the poet just a few lines earlier used to image the vision of the Incarnation. The experience he reports at the end of the *Paradiso* that clove his understanding is the experience that opens the eighth day, traditionally everyman's resurrection day, when the body, the prototype of all images, is glorified.

Now all these examples, which could surely be multiplied,

could do no more than convince one that Dante is a pretty clever poet. But if one takes seriously his claim to be daring a new kind of poetry and, furthermore if one understands him to be displaying what he means in the second canto of the *Paradiso* when he accepts an image from a source other than his own creative genius and allows it to shape his poetry, then Dante appears to be more than a clever poet.

The poetic decision to let one's poetry be shaped by an image that is experienced as received rather than as controlled or contrived parallels the religious decision to let oneself be transformed by an image that opens onto the love that satisfies the heart's desire. Neither decision is comprehensible apart from a fundamental trust in the graciousness of an other to open the way. When Dante is perceived in this way, more beholden than cunning, we can begin to appreciate the significance of the figure of Beatrice. Beatrice above all Dante could not have conjured up. Were there no substance to the forgiving love Beatrice offered Dante, if there were no eyes such as hers animating one face among countless others, Dante would have languished in the wood and the poet would have been compelled to wander, like the modern storyteller, in the wasteland of images he could conjure up. It is Beatrice and the reality of the love Dante perceives in Beatrice that restore the poet's confidence in the essential trustworthiness of the things and people that fill his universe. The more he fixes his senses on them, the more he is drawn out of himself. What marks Dante's poetry in the *Divine Comedy*, then, is not just his attention to the liturgical action of his day, but his attention to all the things and people that happen to ornament his lifetime, an attention that accounts for the precision of his images. The reader is not faced with the awesome burden of "getting inside" a poet like Yeats in order to glimpse a vision; the figures, the gestures, that fill the space of the *Divine Comedy* are figures and gestures familiar to our experience, yet never before so transfigured that, in the woods, they stand out as signposts. Few poets have ever been as attentive to the people, the gestures, the things and the events of life as Dante. But then few were as disposed as Dante to see in them the wellsprings of a new poetic possibility.

CHAPTER 6

Light

There were many other things that Jesus did; if all were written down, the world itself, I suppose, would not hold all the books that would have to be written.[1]

Our exploration of stories told to the dark is nearly over. The attempt to relate different types of stories to different postures of the imagination led us in the first place to distinguish the stories of innocent imagination. These were the stories occasioned by marvelous events or things, told by persons for whom those events or things were matters of life-shaping significance. Whether or not the story was understood literally, it embodied a faith or a conviction that was unshakeable. In this sense the storyteller was *in* his story, personally involved in the event his story celebrated. To question the truth of the story would have been to question the integrity of the storyteller. The white man who ignored the profundity of the resistance of Smohalla's tribe to agriculture not only miscalculated the seriousness of that resistance but was also singularly ignorant of the story *he*, the white man, was in. So it is with the stories we are in. We are almost incapable of seeing around them, so thoroughly are we engrossed in them. We are not unlike the prisoner in Plato's cave, chained to those who share our particular perspective, left to contemplate the shadows, ever tempted to mistake them for realities.

Plato's cave analogy was useful for distinguishing the stories of fallen imagination. These were the stories told by persons who had fallen out of an innocent relation to the things and events of life, whose backs were turned to the shadows. So gnostics of every age turn away from what has a kind of prima facie validity in order to uncover a hidden truth that underlies the appearances, a hidden reality in terms of which everything can be understood. What further distinguished the fallen imagination was its failure to recognize the artificiality of the world it composed when it turned away from the shadows. It saw the figures passing over the bridge and grasped the relation of those figures to the shadows they cast, but it did not see that those figures were man-made. In one regard, fallen imagination was like innocent imagination, in that it was unable to see around the explanation it constructed and accepted for the things and events of life. In place of the shadows, fallen imagination faced its own projections, mistaking them for realities. In the ancient world, the gnostic storyteller projected onto the screen of nature his own psychological processes. In the measure that the story's dominant metaphor, the metaphor of exile, never received critical attention—the kind of attention that can be provided only by someone whose vision embraces other possibilities, by someone who can "see around the story"—the story tended to fix the very person it pretended to free in an illusory world. The more recent historical counterpart to the gnostic is the ideologist. More scientific and theoretical, at least in form, than the gnostic stories, ideological accounts of the things and events of life are every bit as compelling and every bit as confining. The brilliance of the synthesis accounts, at least in part, for the power that the ideology has for many people. In the measure that the intelligent processes that give rise to the synthesis are either ignored or not fully understood, the products of intelligence tend to freeze the person they first freed in a new perspective. Not infrequently the convert to the new perspective holds his former world in contempt. Hence the gnostic in antiquity quite deliberately perverted the most honored stories of the religious tradition from which he had departed; hence the person who rejects his past in favor of a new ideology—whether it be capitalism or communism, fascism or socialism—quite frequently becomes bitter and vociferous in his opposition to what he has left behind, oblivious to the extent to which his life and will are bound by the ideology he now embraces.

The more recent stories of modern fiction, which bear the mark of the storyteller who has both fallen from an innocent relation to the things and events of life and has recognized the artificiality of the fiction he has contrived, emerged then as a third type of story. The modern storyteller, whose imagination is alienated in that moment he becomes self-conscious about his craft, is in a peculiar predicament. If the storyteller inescapably discovers in his stories his own fabrications, if all he sees are artificial figures in the firelight of intelligence that reveal more about himself than about the intended object, he seems compelled to wander in a labyrinth of mirrors. We explored the stories of John Barth and D. H. Lawrence because each of them attempted in his fiction to come to terms with the modern problem of alienation.

Barth, perhaps, best illustrated how the predicament of the storyteller reflects the predicament of children of the Enlightenment. The twentieth-century self-conscious individual beholds a universe that he fully realizes can be put together intelligently in a multitude of ways. His own life lends itself to a multitude of descriptions, a multitude of stories. He is like one located in a funhouse mirror room, his life like a journey through a labyrinth of mirrors. Will any of the mirrors disclose him in his true proportions, offering a way through the maze? Or will he die in the labyrinth, telling stories to the dark? Is there an exit? If there is no exit, why even bother to set out? The storyteller's dilemma is similar. It seems that every conceivable story has been told. What would be the point of offering yet another story if it leads inescapably to the same dead end, if it would be but another mirror in which to see oneself reflected? Barth's way of dealing with the modern predicament is to make it work for him. In recognizing himself in his fictional aspects, in identifying the metaphors that shape the life he is acting out, he manages to drive a wedge between himself and his role. In setting the role apart from himself, he is suddenly free to move in and out of it, just the way the all-knowing author is free to leave Ambrose lost in the funhouse. In much the same way, anyone who can relate to his life-act humorously with a degree of detachment is free to move in and out of roles with alacrity. Still, the dominant funhouse image remains to confine the imagination of artist and person. The artist never imagines that there may ultimately be a way out of the labyrinth. So Barth is more interested in transforming a place of terror and confusion into a place for proper lovers, who, having learned to shed facades like costumes, are free to meet as persons no longer intent on getting on with the story but on enjoying their time together in the dark.

D. H. Lawrence's way of coming to terms with alienation was slightly different. Like Barth, Lawrence did not try to evade the problem but chose to use it to his advantage. He too hoped to move through rather than around the problem of alienation. But unlike Barth, whose fiction offered something like a mirror that reflected all the mirrors, Lawrence seemed intent on finding the kind of mirror he could walk through in order to become possessed of another world. Hence again and again he portrays relationships as involving a recognition of the otherness of the other, a profound experience of the impossibility of reducing the other to one's illusion of the other. Only then, Lawrence suggests, when one has acknowledged the otherness of the other (and, by implication, one's own limits), only then does the other become a threshold into a new world. The deadly moment of alienation must be undergone if there is to be a new birth. So it seems that Lawrence, something like Hegel, imagined a movement beyond the labyrinth of mirrors into the light of day, an emergence from the cave that resembled the infant's emergence from the womb.

Despite their deep differences, the way Barth and Lawrence related to the stories of Scripture perhaps reveals more than anything else the particular bind of alienated imagination. Because the alienated imagination inescapably understands its own products as inventions, as artificial things, its way of relating to others' stories is to transform them, making them its own by making them over. Hence when John Barth writes *Giles Goat-Boy*, his interest in the gospels is limited to the motifs in the life of Jesus that he can pick out and place in relation to motifs present in other stories. He already and always relates to the gospels as a kind of object for dissection and analysis. *Giles Goat-Boy*, a farcical collage of stories, incorporates only those scriptural motifs that contribute to the overall humorous effect Barth hopes to achieve.

D. H. Lawrence, on the other hand, did not relate to the gospels as stories like other stories, products of imagination much like his own. They had a place of greater eminence. But even so, Lawrence did not rest content until he had made them his own, until he had subjected himself to their strangeness only finally to digest them. In digesting them, Lawrence offered in *The Man Who Died* the most profound reading of the gospels of which he was capable. Although Lawrence is admittedly a larger spirit than most, he could not prevent the gospels from shrinking to his own size. Hence while Lawrence can stretch us beyond our own proportions and, consequently, help us to bring a rather larger person to our future reading of the Scriptures, it would be a mistake to allow the Scriptures to be measured by Lawrence.

In turning next to the mystics and to Saint Augustine, we intended to suggest that the way beyond imagination's modern impasse is to refrain from filling the void with imagination, from

breaking the silence either with the stories we are in with a vengeance or with stories we entertain. We learned from the mystics
to be still, to feel afresh the darkness in which our lives are sunk,
and there to wait. When the lake of the heart is quiet, it may be
stirred by something real. So it seemed that Augustine's *Confessions*, as artfully crafted as any of the fictions of the moderns, was
unique in that the lines of the story conformed to the lines of the
life. Furthermore, because the author deliberately refrained from
making over, mindlessly or mindfully, what happened in his life,
he was able to be present to what happened. He was present to
the things and events of his life and they became words that presently broke the silence:

> When first I knew you, you raised me up so that I
> could see that there was something to be seen, but also that I
> was not yet able to see it. I gazed on you with eyes too weak
> to resist the dazzle of your splendour. Your light shone upon
> me in its brilliance, and I thrilled with love and dread alike.
> I realized that I was far away from you. It was as though I
> were in a land where all is different from your own and I
> heard your voice calling from on high, saying "I am the food
> of full-grown men. Grow and you shall feed on me. But you
> shall not change me into your own substance, as you do with
> the food of your body. Instead you shall be changed into
> me."[2]

Augustine's encounter with the Scriptures differed notably from
D. H. Lawrence's. Lawrence digested the Scriptures; *The Man
Who Died* reveals what happens when the "food of full-grown
men" is changed into the substance of one who digests them.
Augustine was transformed by his encounter with the Scriptures.
The more he fed on the Scriptures, the more he came to realize
that "all you asked of me was to deny my own will and accept
yours."[3] Not until Augustine penetrated to the heart of the gospel
story and saw reflected in Christ's humility and obedience the self
to which he was called was his mind "free from the gnawing anx-

ieties of ambition and gain, from wallowing in filth and scratching the itching sore of lust. I began to talk to you freely, O Lord my God, my Light, my Wealth, and my Salvation."⁴ The *Confessions* is the record of his prayer, in which he brings into the presence of his Lord the happenings that until then were lost in the tangle of the everyday. Now the events can speak, and the story they tell *is* the *Confessions*, Augustine's story but also the story of the God who came to stir the waters in the stillness of Augustine's night.

Finally we distinguished the operation of sanctified imagination in Dante's *Divine Comedy*. Augustine suggested that his conversion consisted of a transformation in which his will became one with God's; looking back on his life he realized the obstacles his imagination had placed in his path and called, therefore, for a new asceticism of the imagination. Dante's mind-sundering experience at the end of the *Paradiso* is the identical experience of will and desire moved in accord with the will of God. But Dante finds in the experience the vindication of images. That is not to say that Dante's vision of poetry remains the same as it was before the experience. He warns the reader in the second canto of the *Paradiso* not to embark on the Ocean Dante dares to sail unless he has first "reached up to seize betimes the bread of angels, food for men."⁵ The remark reminds the reader of Augustine's first taste of the divine. The *Divine Comedy* no more than the *Confessions* will diminish the experience of the divine. In the *Divine Comedy*, however, the remark is illustrative in two different yet related ways of the elevated poetic Dante aims to introduce. First, it is significant that the remark takes place in Dante's journey Wednesday of Easter Week. On that day in the Church's celebration of Easter the Offertory of the Mass in Dante's day read:

> The Lord opened the doors of heaven: and he rained down on them manna that they might eat: he gave them the bread of heaven: the bread of angels has man eaten, alleluja.⁶

The image rises from the public, ceremonial context rather than merely at the behest of the innovator; it opens transparently onto the vision of paradise that culminates in Dante's experience of the Incarnation. Second, the remark reminds the reader of the occasion when Dante ate of the bread of angels, at the close of the *Purgatorio*, when raising his beard he saw Beatrice turned toward the Gryphon. It is Beatrice who brings home to Dante the Christian mysteries. When he ascends in contemplation to the center of the revolving spheres, Dante discovers the innermost meaning of the love he knew first in her eyes. If the Christian reality gives that love its substance, the image of Beatrice opens Dante's heart to receive it. True, without the Incarnation, Beatrice would have been another lovely lady to celebrate after the fashion of poets of courtly love. But it is equally true that without Beatrice, the Christian hope would have taken shape neither in Dante's heart nor in the poet's masterpiece. The presence of Beatrice indicates that, in Dante's poetic, the Incarnation saves the appearances, and that images sound divine depths. The eye of the poet who has become still finds unfailingly the signposts in the wood that provoke his exclamation. He is astonishd not so much because he has found a way out as because he perceives that an other has found a way in.

While we have been focusing on the constellations of stories that fill the darkness of our lives, we might as easily turn our attention inward. The journey from dark wood to Light that powers the stars, from stories told to the dark to the radiant source of all our imaginings is, after all, our journey as much as it is Dante's.

We have none of us been spared the agonies and ecstasies of childhood. Once upon a time pillows were clouds, or clouds pillows. We never doubted for a moment the truth of the story our folks passed on to us, however fantastic it may have sounded, however little we fathomed its meanings. The more remarkable thing is that stories, like children, should ever grow up and lose some of the innocence that belongs properly only to children.

When childhood passes, the stories of childhood recede. They become part of the baggage that tends to get left behind as one grows older and wiser in the ways of the world. If once we were as attached to them as to the folks who first told them to us, our distance from them grows as we learn to step out on our own. The further we move away from our folks, the more their tales get lost in the din and confusion of adolescence. The momentum of the life picks up dramatically as in youth we plunge into one experience after another that opens up world upon world even as it closes the door behind to childhood and innocence. We become saturated with experiences that we have neither time nor inclination to sort out. We go on hardly knowing why or where until one day our flying carpet slips out from under us and we fall down, down, down grasping wildly for something to hold on to. The death of someone we love, a serious injury, the necessity of making a life decision—something that compels attention—puts before us Alfie's question, What's it all about? We will never be more susceptible to the gnostic or ideologist who panders solutions to all life's riddles. If we fall into their stories, the blur of the past yields to the dark blacks and whites of the present. What in adolescence we never understood about our experiences is suddenly clear. Armed with the Truth, we venture out into the World.

But the World receives us not. It has seen our kind before. It returns to us the Truth we intended to lay on it and many more besides. As it dawns on us that ours is a many-storied universe reaching to heights of which we had not dreamed, our feeling of dislocation makes our earlier tumbling seem like child's play. It isn't as we then felt, that there was no sense to be made of our adolescent experiences; the trouble is that too much sense can be made of them. In every direction we turn there is another diagnosis of our condition. Whose are we to accept? In our night sky there are so many stars that shine. How in the world are we to take our bearings? It is this question, I think, that identifies the contemporary point of departure. It most assuredly inspired our present exploration of stories told to the dark. In searching through the stories people have told throughout the ages, it occurred to me that the contemporary question may also have been Augustine's question. He, at least, more than anyone else, pointed a way to go. Fall still, he seemed to counsel, don't let your imagination light up the sky like a sun. Fall still and let the stars come out. Then take a good look at your night sky. See where the stars are and let your description be faithful to what you see. It was as if Augustine were saying that, sure, there are a lot of stories (here's another), but the only one that really matters is the one that lies in the lake of your heart. Quiet down a bit and you'll see that story reflected in your own night sky. To the question, "how will we know we are really discovering the story that lies in the lake of the heart?" Augustine's reply must be, "if you have become still, the lake of your heart will be stirred by things that are real. The stars will come out in your night sky. But you must be still."

Were we to examine our night sky, we might, like Dante, find one star among the many that holds our attention. Our movement to it would involve our willingness to overcome the resistances that lie deep within, our willingness to shed our illusions and conceits as we catch ourselves in one story or another up Purgatory's mountain, and finally our opening to the love that has been offered it in the pouring out of another life centuries ago. No one of us could have compelled that act. The desolate ignore it. Those in the dark are drawn to it. Those in love overflow with it. They will not be still. John was a prophet when he finished his gospel with the words:

> There were many other things that Jesus did; if all were written down, the world itself, I suppose, would not hold all the books that would have to be written.[7]

Dante was not the first, nor will he be the last, to break the silence.

Notes

Introduction
   1. Rainer Maria Rilke, *Stories of God*, tr. by M. D. Herter Norton (New York: W. W. Norton & Company, Inc., 1963), p. 127.

Chapter 1
   1. James Mooney, "The Ghost-Dance Religion, and the Sioux Outbreak of 1890" in the *Annual Report of the Bureau of American Ethnology XIV*, 2, Washington, 1896 (pp. 641-1136), p. 721.
   2. For an excellent summary of Eliade's position, see his "Methodological Remarks on the Study of Religious Symbolism" in *The History of Religions*, ed. Mircea Eliade and Joseph Kitagawa (Chicago: University of Chicago Press, 1959), pp. 86-107.
   3. One of my wife Karen's unpublished poems amplifies better than I could my meaning:

> To catch a word, a single word—
> Like trying to hold the
> fountain's water in a cup of hands,
> Or still a drop of ocean spray.
>
> I am washed, washed by water and words,
> And ridiculously small and fragile
> Am filled by the boundless water and word.
>
> Dazzled, drenched dreamer
> Dreaming
> Longing, laughing, weeping,
> Shouting my word,
> Faintest whisper heard,
>
> Back to the sea
> Which gave it to me
>
> To the sea of All Words and All Silence,
> Back to the singing sea.

   4. Alexander Heidel, *The Babylonian Genesis*, second edition (Chicago: The University of Chicago Press, 1951), p. 18. Parentheses indicate where text is corrupt.
   5. *Ibid.*
   6. *Ibid.*, p. 19.
   7. *Ibid.*
   8. *Ibid.*, p. 29.

9. *Ibid.*, p. 36.

10. *Ibid.*, pp. 40-41.

11. *Ibid.*, p. 46.

12. *Ibid.*, p. 48.

13. The philosopher of religion must marvel at how economically the storyteller relates here the death of a god.

14. Such passages convince the liturgist that the *Enuma Elish* was not only recited but enacted.

15. Cf. Gabriel Marcel, *The Mystery of Being*, Vol. 1 (Chicago: Henry Regnery Company, 1960), p. 260.

16. Jacques Maritain, *Creative Intuition in Art and Poetry*, Bollingen Edition (New York: Pantheon Books, Inc., 1953), p. 180, fn. 33.

17. *Genesis* 2:5-9.

18. Paul Ricoeur, *The Symbolism of Evil* (New York: Harper & Row, 1967), p. 234.

19. *Genesis* 3:12.

20. *Genesis* 3:13.

21. *Genesis* 3:5-6.

Chapter 2

1. *Kephalaia*, ed. and tr. H. J. Polotsky and A. Böhlig, (Oxford: Oxford University Press) Ch. 1, 14:29-15:24; cited in Hans Jonas, *The Gnostic Religion*, second edition, revised (Boston: Beacon Press, 1963), pp. 208-209. My emphasis.

2. *Ibid.*

3. Plato, *The Dialogues of Plato*, trans. B. Jowett (Boston and New York: The Jefferson Press, 1871), pp. 841-842.

4. *The Gnostic Religion*, p. 209.

5. Karl Marx, *A Contribution to the Critique of Political Economy*, trans. N. I. Stone (Chicago: Charles H. Kerr & Company, 1904), pp. 11-12.

6. *The Gnostic Religion*, p. 209.

7. Sigmund Freud, *The Future of an Illusion*, tr. W. D. Robson-Scott, ed. J. Strachey (New York: Doubleday & Company, Inc., 1964), p. 35.

8. *Ibid.*, p. 47.

9. J. H. Newman, *Grammar of Assent* (New York: Doubleday & Company, Inc., 1955), p. 101.

10. G. M. Hopkins, *Poems and Prose*, ed. W. H. Gardner (Baltimore: Penguin, 1953), p. 27.

11. *The Gnostic Religion*, pp. 113-116.

12. The phrase, taken from C. S. Lewis's *Till We Have Faces; a Myth Retold* (Grand Rapids: William B. Eerdmans Publishing Company, 1966), refers to the myth in which Psyche must descend into the underworld to fetch the beauty of Persephone, the Queen of the Dead.

13. The life of the deadlands is the life of those who will someday die but whose refusal to face up to the fact makes of their life a living death.

14. Joanne Marxhausen and Dan Johnson, *Thank God for Circles* (Minneapolis: Augsburg Publishing House, 1971).

15. Flannery O'Connor, *Mystery and Manners*, ed. Sally and Robert Fitzgerald (New York: Farrer, Straus & Giroux, 1961), p. 35.

16. Whereas the Gnostic regards this world in purely negative terms, the Christian hastens to affirm the world as God's creation. Whereas the Gnostic regards life on earth as imprisonment, the Christian sees life as a pilgrimage.

17. *The Gnostic Religion*, p. 209.

18. In one version of the story, the mechanism for removing Light was a water wheel. By means of the wheel, particles of Light would be transferred to the moon. The waxing of the moon was the visible sign of the movement of the Light. The waning of the moon signified the passing on of the Light to the sun itself along the Milky Way. Hence, the visible universe was but a sacrament of the spiritual reality of the ongoing process of redemption, of the return home to the source of Light of souls in exile.

19. The foregoing is a summary of a sketch presented by Hans Jonas in *The Gnostic Religion*, pp. 206-237.

20. *Ibid.*, p. 209.

21. Augustine, *Confessions*, ed. R. S. Pine-Coffin (Baltimore: Penguin, 1961), p. 94. My emphasis.

22. *Ibid.*, p. 103.

23. *Ibid.*, p. 88. My emphasis.

Chapter 3

1. John Barth, *Lost in the Funhouse* (New York: Bantam Books, Inc., 1969), pp. 81-82, 91-92.

2. Immanuel Kant, *Critique of Pure Reason*, tr. N. K. Smith (New York: St. Martin's Press, 1965), pp. 21-22.

3. Kant's proposal that space and time are internal ordering principles is, at first, strange and difficult to accept. It is at least as strange to us as Copernicus' suggestion that the earth moved was to the people of his day. Common sense seems to counsel otherwise, that space is something "out there" in which things are located. Yet we do not see space the way we might see a tree. We say the tree is *in* space, but what do we mean? The more such questions are considered, the more convincing Kant's hypothesis becomes, even to common sense.

When more recent scientific evidence is considered, Kant's case becomes even more impressive. The space we occupy, the space we move through when we go somewhere, is Euclidean three-dimensional space. Euclidean geometry, however, is far from the only geometry conceivable. Others have been proposed and, in fact, another is *applied* in plotting the path of satellites and in determining where to locate the ships to recover astronauts. If space were something "out there," we would not need more than one geometry to map it. As it is, the lives of astronauts depend upon the development of a non-Euclidean geometry and a different conception of space from the one we ordinarily employ. Newton was aware of the problem of the relativity of spatial frames of reference and attempted to discover Absolute Space, an absolute frame of reference. What Newton was looking for "outside," Kant located within in terms sufficiently general to accommodate different geometries, though he seems to have contemplated only Euclidean geometry. Hence space was for Kant one of the conditions of possibility for the organization of sensations into perceptions.

4. There is nothing unreasonable about Kant's postulate. Once he had supposed that objects must conform to our knowledge, that what is known is necessarily something in relation to a knower, he could not avoid conceiving of the known as phenomena—that which shows itself to a knower. Once he had done that, there was a logical exigence to distinguish things-in-relation (phenomena) from things-in-themselves (noumena).

5. Friederich Nietzsche, *Nietzsche's Werke.* Band V: *Die Fröhliche Wissenschaft* (Leipzig: C. G. Naumann, 1900), pp. 163-164. My translation; my emphasis.

6. *Ibid.*

7. *Ibid.*

8. *Ibid.*

9. G.W.F. Hegel, *Phänomenologie des Geistes in Sämtliche Werke.* Band II (Leipzig: Felix Meiner, 1937), pp. 128-129 (*my translation*).

10. In science, the introduction of a variety of measuring devices calculated to reduce the effect of the subject becomes standard procedure. While people may disagree about a color's hue, there is remarkable agreement about a color's wavelength. In the humanities, considerable effort is expended to bracket one's own questions and concerns in order to hear the other's more accurately.

11. Soren Kierkegaard, *Concluding Unscientific Postscript*, tr. D. F. Swenson and W. Lowrie (Princeton: Princeton University Press, 1941), p. 18.

12. *Lost in the Funhouse*, pp. 81-82.

13. D. H. Lawrence, *The Rainbow* (New York: The Viking Press, 1961), p. 1.

14. *Ibid.*, p. 2.

15. *Ibid.*

16. *Ibid.*, p. 3.

17. *Ibid.*, p. 7.

18. *Ibid.*, p. 36.

19. *Ibid.*, p. 14.

20. *Ibid.*

21. *Ibid.*, p. 46.

22. *Ibid.*, p. 49.

23. *Ibid.*, pp. 50-51.

24. *Ibid.*, p. 60.

25. *Ibid.*, p. 78.

26. *Ibid.*

27. *Ibid.*, p. 90.

28. *Ibid.*, pp. 91-92.
29. *Ibid.*, p. 256.
30. *Ibid.*, p. 115.
31. *Ibid.*
32. *Ibid.*, p. 116.
33. *Ibid.*
34. *Ibid.*, p. 118.
35. *Ibid.*, p. 119.
36. *Ibid.*, p. 36.
37. *Ibid.*, p. 176.
38. *Ibid.*, p. 171.
39. *Ibid.*
40. *Ibid.*, p. 166.
41. *Ibid.*, pp. 140-141.
42. *Ibid.*, p. 141.
43. *Ibid.*, p. 147.
44. *Ibid.*, p. 148.
45. *Ibid.*, pp. 149-150.
46. *Ibid.*, p. 146.
47. *Ibid.*, p. 171.
48. *Ibid.*, p. 176.
49. *Ibid.*, p. 179.
50. *Ibid.*, pp. 180-181.
51. *Ibid.*, p. 183.
52. *Ibid.*, p. 184.
53. *Ibid.*, pp. 186-187.
54. *Ibid.*, pp. 192-193.
55. *Ibid.*, pp. 316-317.
56. *Ibid.*, p. 320.
57. *Ibid.*, p. 493.
58. *Ibid.*, p. 494.
59. *Ibid.*
60. D. H. Lawrence, *The Man Who Died* (New York: Vintage Books, 1953), p. 167.
61. *Ibid.*, p. 168.
62. *Ibid.*, p. 169.
63. *Ibid.*, p. 173.
64. *Ibid.*
65. *Ibid.*
66. *Ibid.*, p. 174.
67. *Ibid.*, p. 184.
68. *Ibid.*, p. 188.
69. *Ibid.*, pp. 189-190.
70. *Ibid.*, p. 196.
71. *Ibid.*, p. 200.
72. *Ibid.*, p. 201.

73. *Ibid.*, p. 203.
74. *Ibid.*, p. 204.
75. *Ibid.*
76. *Ibid.*
77. *Ibid.*, pp. 204-205.
78. *Ibid.*, p. 206.
79. *Ibid.*
80. *Ibid.*, p. 208.
81. *Lost in the Funhouse*, p. 3. My emphasis.
82. *Ibid.*
83. *Ibid.*, p. 36.
84. *Ibid.*, p. 54.
85. *Ibid.*, p. 69.
86. *Ibid.*
87. *Ibid.*
88. *Ibid.*, p. 74.
89. *Ibid.*, p. 76.
90. *Ibid.*, p. 86.
91. *Ibid.*, pp. 84-85.
92. *Ibid.*, p. 86.
93. *Ibid.*
94. *Ibid.*
95. *Ibid.*, p. 87.
96. *Ibid.*
97. *Ibid.*, p. 74.
98. *Ibid.*, p. 90.
99. *Ibid.*
100. *Ibid.*, p. 91.
101. *Ibid.*, p. 92.
102. *Ibid.*
103. *Ibid.*, pp. 93-94.
104. *Ibid.*, p. 113.
105. *Ibid.*
106. *Ibid.*, pp. 113-114.
107. *Ibid.*, p. 114.
108. *Ibid.*
109. *Ibid.*, pp. 115-116.
110. *Ibid.*, p. 116.
111. *Ibid.*
112. *Ibid.*
113. *Ibid.*, p. 126.
114. *Ibid.*, pp. 125-126.
115. *Ibid.*, p. 93.

Chapter 4
1. *The Cloud of Unknowing*, tr. C. Wolters (Baltimore: Penguin Books, 1961), pp. 54, 65.

2. Annie Dillard, *Pilgrim at Tinker Creek* (New York: Harper's Magazine Press, 1974), p. 258.

3. *Ibid.*

4. *Ibid.*, p. 259.

5. *Ibid.*

6. *The Cloud of Unknowing*, p. 58.

7. Helen Waddell, *The Desert Fathers* (Ann Arbor: The University of Michigan Press, 1957), p. 63.

8. *Ibid.*

9. *Confessions*, p. 46.

10. *Ibid.*, p. 78.

11. *Ibid.*, p. 77.

12. *Ibid.*, p. 61.

13. *Ibid.*, pp. 61-62.

14. *Ibid.*, p. 147.

15. *Ibid.*, p. 21.

16. *Ibid.*, p. 290.

17. *Ibid.*, p. 281.

18. *Ibid.*, p. 156.

19. *Pilgrim at Tinker Creek*, p. 69.

20. *Ibid.*, p. 62.

Chapter 5

1. Dante Alighieri, *The Divine Comedy 3, Paradiso*, tr. D. Sayers and B. Reynolds (Baltimore: Penguin Books, 1962) 2:1-15.

2. *Ibid.*, 2:7.

3. *Ibid.*, 2:7-8.

4. *Ibid.*, 1:13-14.

5. *Ibid.*, 1:46-54.

6. Dante Alighieri, *The Divine Comedy 2, Purgatorio*, tr. D. Sayers (Baltimore: Penguin Books, 1955) 33:101.

7. *Paradiso*, 1:22-24.

8. Hereafter, in order to keep clear the distinction between Dante the poet and Dante the pilgrim and main character of the poem, we will refer to the pilgrim as "Dante" and the poet as "the poet." The poet occupies the vantage point of "sanctified imagination." The pilgrim is portrayed as being on the way.

9. Dante Alighieri, *The Divine Comedy 1, Inferno*, tr. D. Sayers (Baltimore: Penguin Books, 1949) 1:2-3.

10. *Ibid.*, 1:11.

11. *Ibid.*, 1:12.

12. *Ibid.*, 1:19-21.

13. *The Desert Fathers*, p. 63.

14. *Inferno*, 1:49-60.

15. *Inferno*, p. 75.

16. Theologically, Dante has preserved the orthodox insistence that God's grace saves (Virgil is sent ultimately by everyman's intercessor, Mary—he

could not have been conjured up by Dante) while it leaves man's freedom intact (Dante is free to reject Virgil).

17. *Inferno*, 34:10-12.

18. *Ibid.*, 34:25.

19. *Ibid.*, 34:61-69.

20. *Ibid.*, 34:88-90.

21. *Ibid.*, 34:104.

22. Cf. *Inferno*, p. 291: "When Satan fell from Heaven, two things happened. (1) The dry land, which until then had occupied the Southern Hemisphere, fled in horror from before him, and fetched up in the Northern Hemisphere; while the ocean poured in from all sides to fill the gap. (2) The inner bowels of the Earth, to avoid contact with him, rushed upwards towards the south, and there formed the island and mountain at the top of which was the Earthly Paradise, ready for the reception of Man, and which, after Hell's Harrowing became Mount Purgatory. This, according to Dante, is the only land in the Southern Hemisphere. The hollow thus left in the middle of the Earth is the core of Hell, together with the space in which Dante and Virgil are now standing—the "tomb" of Satan. From this a winding passage leads up to the surface of the Antipodes. By this passage the river Lethe descends, and up it the poets now make their way.

23. *Ibid.*, 34:134.

24. *Ibid.*, 34:139.

25. *Purgatorio*, 9:30.

26. *Ibid.*, 9:40.

27. *Ibid.*, 9:94-102.

28. *Ibid.*, p. 139.

29. *Ibid.*, 10:43-45.

30. *Ibid.*, 11:133-138.

31. *Ibid.*, 11:142.

32. Even when Dante takes his place among those who are being purged of the vices believed to have been Dante's, he seems more to be going through the motions ritually than to be really experiencing release from the images that hold him back. The movement is more like the symbolic ascent of the steps to Saint Peter's Gate than the real experience of being purged, crushed, and opened.

33. Cf. above, fn. 22.

34. *Purgatorio*, 27:49-51.

35. *Ibid.*, 27:52-54.

36. *Ibid.*, 27:8.

37. *Ibid.*, 30:73-74.

38. *Ibid.*, 30:76-78.

39. *Ibid.*, 30:107-108.

40. *Ibid.*, 30:121-126, 129, 130, 133-135, 136-138, 142-145.

41. *Ibid.*, 31:5-6, 11-12.

42. *Ibid.*, 31:13-14.

43. *Ibid.*, 31:19.

44. *Ibid.*, p. 139.
45. *Ibid.*, 31:80-81.
46. *Ibid.*, 31:82-89.
47. *Ibid.*, 31:94-96, 100-102.
48. *Ibid.*, 31:118-126.
49. *Ibid.*, 31:137-138.
50. *Ibid.*, 32:34-51.
51. *Ibid.*, 32:58-60.
52. *Ibid.*, 32:48.
53. *Ibid.*, 33:101.
54. *Paradiso*, 2:1-2.
55. *Ibid.*, 2:10-13.
56. *Missale Romanum*, second edition (Cincinnati: Benziger Brothers, Inc., 1942), p. 340.
57. *Paradiso*, 6:11-12.
58. *Ibid.*, 9:32-33.
59. *Ibid.*, 10:94-96.
60. *Ibid.*, 5:118-119.
61. *Ibid.*, 3:70-72, 85.
62. *Ibid.*, 32:4-15.
63. *Ibid.*, 32:19-21.
64. *Ibid.*, 32:55-66.
65. *Ibid.*, 33:25-27.
66. *Ibid.*, 33:55-63.
67. *Ibid.*, 33:71.
68. *Ibid.*, 33:82-87, 97-105.
69. *Ibid.*, 33:112-120, 127-132.
70. *Ibid.*, 33:136-145.
71. *Ibid.*, 33:143.
72. *Ibid.*, 2:10-13.
73. *Ibid.*, 2:10-11.

Chapter 6
1. John 21:25.
2. *Confessions*, p. 147.
3. *Ibid.*, p. 81.
4. *Ibid.*
5. *Paradiso*, 2:10-11.
6. *Missale Romanum*, p. 340.
7. John 21:25.